Rediscovering Lewis

Rediscovering Lewis

Edited by
IAN S. MARKHAM
ANDREW LAZO

PICKWICK *Publications* • Eugene, Oregon

REDISCOVERING LEWIS

Copyright © 2025 Ian S. Markham and Andrew Lazo. All rights reserved. Except for brief quotations in critical publications or reviews, no part of this book may be reproduced in any manner without prior written permission from the publisher. Write: Permissions, Wipf and Stock Publishers, 199 W. 8th Ave., Suite 3, Eugene, OR 97401.

Pickwick Publications
An Imprint of Wipf and Stock Publishers
199 W. 8th Ave., Suite 3
Eugene, OR 97401

www.wipfandstock.com

PAPERBACK ISBN: 979-8-3852-4154-5
HARDCOVER ISBN: 979-8-3852-4155-2
EBOOK ISBN: 979-8-3852-4156-9

Cataloguing-in-Publication data:

Names: Markham, Ian S. [editor] | Lazo, Andrew [editor].

Title: Rediscovering Lewis / edited by Ian S. Markham and Andrew Lazo.

Description: Eugene, OR: Pickwick Publications, 2025 | Includes bibliographical references.

Identifiers: ISBN 979-8-3852-4154-5 (paperback) | ISBN 979-8-3852-4155-2 (hardcover) | ISBN 979-8-3852-4156-9 (ebook)

Subjects: LCSH: Lewis, C. S. (Clive Staples), 1898–1963 | Lewis, C. S. (Clive Staples), 1898–1963—Religion

Classification: PR6023 M37 2025 (print) | PR6023 (ebook)

All rights reserved. No part of this publication may be reproduced, distributed, or transmitted in any form or by any means, including photocopying, recording, or other electronic or mechanical methods, without the prior written permission of the publisher, except in the case of brief quotations embodied in critical reviews and certain other noncommercial uses permitted by copyright law.

Permission Statement and Bible Ascriptions

"To Charles Williams" by C. S. Lewis is copyright © C. S. Lewis Pte. Ltd. Reprinted by permission.

Scripture quotations marked KJV are from the King James or Authorized Version.

Scripture quotations marked NRSV are from the New Revised Standard Version, copyright © 1989, Division of Christian Education of the National Council of the Churches of Christ in the United States of America. Used by permission. All rights reserved.

To Walter Hooper and to the ongoing legacy
of Virginia Theological Seminary

Contents

Acknowledgments ix

Introduction | *Ian S. Markham and Andrew Lazo* | xi

Suffering Is God's Megaphone | *Patrick P. Augustine* | 1

Perichoretic Hymnody: *Perelandra* as Model for Theological Poetics | *Junius Johnson* | 23

"Joy Silenced Me": Sarah Coakley's *Théologie Totale* in C. S. Lewis's Work and Thought | *Andrew Lazo* | 38

"But Only Say the Word, and I Shall Be Healed": Conversion in the Writings of C. S. Lewis | *Tricia Lyons* | 60

C. S. Lewis, Natural Theology, and Anglicanism | *Ian S. Markham* | 77

"Oh Unless It Were You": C. S. Lewis and the Poetry of Friendship | *Karen Swallow Prior* | 93

Truth and Narrative: C. S. Lewis on the Atonement as a Paradigm for Careful Listening | *Jane Williams* | 114

Acknowledgments

ALL BOOKS ARE A journey. This book was partly born in COVID. It was a gift to think beyond the immediate crisis of our season and remind ourselves of the eternal themes of the gospel. The two editors enjoyed many a moment of glad and engaging conversation as we shared our mutual admiration for C. S. Lewis.

Christina Boyd assisted with the numerous logistics of the conference. Robin Parry saw the significance of the project and has been an attentive commissioning editor. John Knight and Beth Clarke offered invaluable aid at the earliest and latest stages of the project. A number of interlocutors, including Ryan Danker and Cherie Harder, lent their time to add valuable insight and affirmation. And we have not nearly enough space to acknowledge the countless ways that the great work and bright cheer of Taryn Habberly continues to move all good things forward. We thank God for them all.

Finally, we are deeply grateful to our respective wives—Lesley and Christin—who continue to support, guide, believe in, and love us through the many projects that consume our time.

Ian S. Markham and Andrew Lazo

Introduction

By Ian S. Markham and Andrew Lazo

PERHAPS HE IS ONE of the most influential theologians of our age. C. S. Lewis (1898–1963) would be surprised. He was, after all, first and foremost a literary critic and historian, and professor of English literature. He was a reluctant convert to Christianity. Yet he continues to enjoy a considerable following among American Evangelicals; everyone from Billy Graham to Max Lucado have quoted approvingly from Lewis. Among the Roman Catholics, Pope Benedict XVI quoted Lewis's *Surprised by Joy* in his *Jesus of Nazareth*, and St. Pope John Paul II in his *Theology of the Body* quoted significantly from Lewis's *The Four Loves*. And there has been endless speculation on why Lewis did not convert to the Roman Catholic Church.[1] Yet Lewis was always an Anglican. A number of his positions would surprise many Evangelicals and Roman Catholics. He held a rather skeptical view about the inerrancy of Scripture; he argued for the possibility that some animals might be immortal; his view of the atonement was complex and neither completely traditional nor fully developed.

In recent decades, the Episcopal Church has taken the theme of justice as central to our witness. This is right and proper. As a church deeply tainted by the association with empire and power,

---

1. Benedict XVI, *Jesus of Nazareth*, 271; John Paul II, *Theology of the Body*, 145. See Petiprin, "C. S. Lewis." It was Joseph Pearce in his book *C. S. Lewis and the Catholic Church* who provoked the debate about why Lewis did not convert given his deep affinity in belief. Petiprin notes that Lewis has attracted many Roman Catholic admirers, including Bishop Robert Barron and St. Pope John Paul II.

we recognize and grapple with the fact that in key ways we have fallen far short as true disciples of the Christ of peace, love, and justice. Yet we as Episcopalians are not just another secular outreach ministry. We frame our convictions around justice on the conviction that at the heart of the universe is goodness and love enabling and sustaining everything that is. Like the eighth-century prophets of the Hebrew Bible, the call for justice is grounded in the recognition that transcending every human community and culture is a God who requires us "to act justly, to love faithfulness, and to walk humbly with your God" (Micah 6:8). Our blend of theological thoughtfulness and justice orientation can, we believe, be grounded helpfully and thoughtfully in the work of C. S. Lewis. Hence, we offer this collection of essays, both to grapple with some of the implications of the questions of justice and also to discharge a duty of justice to Lewis, whose position is sometimes overlooked or undervalued, despite his ongoing influence on readers worldwide.

The Genesis of This Book

Like many things that matter, this book began in a place: Alexandria, Virginia, at the top of Seminary Hill, at Virginia Theological Seminary, poised to mark its bicentenary in 2023. Over coffee, the editors dreamed aloud about a colloquium to mark the moment, and it seemed to them fitting to explore the work of C. S. Lewis. Our working title was "Still Speaking: C. S. Lewis as Theologian for the Third Millennium," a way to grapple with the complex legacy of that key figure of the twentieth century. Lewis himself enjoyed a slim connection to the seminary: Walter Hooper, who served as secretary to Lewis in the final months of his life, had attended VTS briefly before finding his vocation in promoting and preserving the legacy of Lewis.

And so, in late April 2023, we gathered about a dozen contributors and interlocutors from a wide array of backgrounds in the newly-renovated deanery to grapple with the complex implications of a complex figure. We did not always agree—but we had

INTRODUCTION

designed it that way. Before gathering, we had exchanged and read drafts of each others' essays, preparing ourselves for that kind of conversation that Lewis and his friends the Inklings must have enjoyed as they gathered in Lewis rooms to discuss their works in progress. A teenaged Lewis once remarked to his lifelong friend Arthur Greeves that "when one has read a book, I think there is nothing so nice as discussing it with someone else—even though it sometimes produces rather fierce arguments," a sentiment we echoed in our time together.[2] Because we had gathered such a collegial group, we found we enjoyed and profited even from the arguments. Inklings scholar Diana Pavlac Glyer looks at Lewis and his friends through the lens of intellectual hospitality—that gift of presenting our own perspectives and engaging the ideas of others with a kind of academic charity that offers such a hopeful and helpful place in a world marked by increased intolerance. We found that Lewis brought us all together, offering us a chance to understand a wide array of ideas other than our own. We relished the opportunity, to engage with each other, to re-evaluate our own work and now, finally to offer you the results of our efforts. We had from the start, and continue to have, the sense that Lewis would have heartily enjoyed this project we now present; we invite you to continue the conversation about how Lewis is still speaking, and how rediscovering his life and work offers ideas worth embracing.

Our contributors come from a wide array of places, geographical, denominational, and intellectual. Anglican Bishop Patrick P. Augustine, a native of Pakistan, serves in South Sudan for much of the year, but regularly makes his home in many places: Florida, Wisconsin, Oxford, and wherever else he can serve. His essay explores the ideas of suffering he finds both in Lewis and in his own global ministry. Independent scholar Junius Johnson attended both Oral Roberts and Yale, and offers insightful perspectives about theological poetics, especially as he discovers them in Lewis's science fiction. Andrew Lazo combines a lifetime as a Lewis scholar with his experience as an Episcopal priest to read Lewis's work in light of Anglican theology, engaging especially

2. Lewis, *Collected Letters*, 1:173.

INTRODUCTION

with Sarah Coakley's *thèologie totale*. Harvard-trained Tricia Lyons, a priest and VTS professor, takes up the long-overdue task of exploring the idea of conversion in Lewis's fiction, drawing important conclusions about how conversion operates in and on us. Ian S. Markham, the English dean of an important American seminary, brings years of scholarship to bear in his discussion of Lewis's apologetics relate to natural theology, and in so doing reasserts an Anglican theological claim upon Lewis. Karen Swallow Prior brings a wealth of literary teaching, writing, and thinking from within Southern Baptist perspectives to read closely a crucial poem by Lewis about fellow Inkling Charles Williams, and in so doing explores the poetry of friendship with far-reaching implications. And Anglican theologian Jane Williams traveled from the Welsh home she shares with husband Rowan Williams to dive deeply into the way Lewis's approaches to the Holy Trinity can offer us ways to listen to each other with love—a timely call indeed.

It was a joy to explore these ideas in solitude, to present them in fellowship, and now to release them with hope—a hope that Lewis shared about the exchange of ideas that can point us ultimately to faith, hope, and love in our everyday experience of God.

Benedict XVI. *Jesus of Nazareth: From the Baptism in the Jordan to the Transfiguration*. San Francisco: Ignatius, 2008.
John Paul II. *The Theology of the Body: Human Love in the Divine Plan*. Boston: Pauline, 1997.
Lewis, C. S. *Collected Letters*. 3 vols. Edited by Walter Hooper. San Francisco: HarperSanFrancisco, 2004.
Pearce, Joseph. *C. S. Lewis and the Catholic Church*. Charlotte, NC: Saint Benedict, 2013.
Petiprin, Andre. "C. S. Lewis: A Mere Catholic?" Word on Fire, Dec. 30, 2019. https://www.wordonfire.org/articles/fellows/c-s-lewis-a-mere-catholic/.

1

Suffering Is God's Megaphone

Patrick P. Augustine

[Prayers in time of anguish] are themselves a form of anguish. Some people feel guilty about their anxieties and regard them as a defect of faith. I don't agree at all. They are afflictions, not sins. Like all afflictions, they are, if we can so take them, our share in the Passion of Christ. For the beginning of the Passion—the first move, so to speak—is in Gethsemane. . . .[T]he prayer in Gethsemane shows that the preceding anxiety is equally God's will and equally part of our human destiny.[1]

C. S. Lewis is one of the twentieth century's most famous and recognizable figures. A man of vast intellect, a Christian scholar, apologist, storyteller, and inspirational writer. Pope John Paul II singled him out with high praise as a masterful defender of the faith.[2] During World War II, he gave talks on BBC radio, a source of faith and hope. His voice in Britain became a most-recognized voice, and Winston Churchill offered him a special medal after the war. He was on the cover of *Time* magazine on September 8, 1947. He is commemorated on November 22 in the calendar of saints of the Episcopal Church in the United States of America. He wrote

---

1. Lewis, *Letters to Malcolm*, 41–42, 43.

2. Turley, "Remembering C. S. Lewis," s.vv. "An American Converts in Oxford."

forty books in his lifetime, alongside numerous other shorter pieces. His influence has spread worldwide as his books have been translated into over thirty languages. Even in just the first twenty years of the twenty-first century, annual sales of Lewis's books are approaching six million copies. Many of his most popular works have been made into films and movies. And since he died in 1963, hundreds of works have been created that explore Lewis's life and his ideas. Clearly, he has an enduring legacy that intrigues and inspires people well into the third millennium.

Why is Lewis so compelling and popular? First, Lewis's life and writings speak to an incredible array of people. His life, the story of a doubting atheist who became a champion of Christianity, speaks to anyone who has struggled with doubt and issues of faith. Similarly, his writings connect with people who range from children captivated by the dazzling imaginative world of Narnia to adults who want to learn more about the Christian faith in *Mere Christianity*. Second, his appeal is not limited to the library shelves reserved for the intellectual or imaginative because he addresses the full spectrum of human experiences: Lewis addresses the search for a deep happiness and his conversion to Christianity in *Surprised by Joy*, he writes about pain and despair in *The Problem of Pain*, and he talks about the gradual loss of faith in *The Screwtape Letters* and *The Pilgrim's Regress*. Third, Lewis's approach is very resonant because guiding all his works is his lived experience. Pain, joy, sorrow, doubt, happiness, and faith are vividly explored, not just as ideas but as parts of life.

This willingness to write about the different experiences that make up human life most contributes to Lewis's enduring appeal. These experiences are not just restricted to an Anglo-Irish Oxbridge academic but are shared by everyone. As a missionary bishop, I have served the poorest of the poor, Christians who live in Pakistan and South Sudan, and people whose lives are very different and very removed from Oxford. I have seen firsthand that, despite vast differences, Lewis's ideas speak to everyone, from the wealthiest and most affluent in England and the United States to destitute South Sudanese refugees. Regardless of background, we all experience suffering, loss, and joy. What Lewis describes touches on the realities of the ever-present and ever-living God. As Ps 139 says:

> You go before me and follow me. You place your hand of blessing on my head. Such knowledge is too wonderful for me, too great for me to understand! I can never escape from your Spirit! I can never get away from your presence! If I go up to heaven, you are there; if I go down to the grave, you are there. If I ride the wings of the morning, if I dwell by the farthest oceans, Even there your hand will guide me, and your strength will support me. I could ask the darkness to hide me and the light around me to become night—but even in darkness I cannot hide from you. To you the night shines as bright as day. Darkness and light are the same to you. (Ps 139:5–12)

As Lewis captures in his writings, there is no place, no way that God is not a part of our experiences. In the desolation of the South Sudanese refugee camps or the griminess of an isolated and lonely Christian cemetery in Pakistan, God is ever present.

For many people, in both Lewis's time and our own, the pain and suffering in the world is evidence of a nonexistent or, at best, disinterested God. A part of Lewis's enduring appeal is that he fully confronts these questions about suffering and God. Rather than trivialize concerns, Lewis addresses the problem of pain. For Lewis, pain and suffering are the principal ways that people can rediscover the ever-present God. The issue is so vital that Lewis devotes an entire book, *The Problem of Pain*, to addressing the issue of pain and suffering. Pain, along with all experiences, has a theological component, one that is rooted in God's presence in the world. According to Lewis, God shapes and forms us through our experiences, including pain and suffering. Pain draws our attention to God, whether we desire it or not. As Lewis writes, "God whispers to us in our pleasures, speaks in our conscience, but shouts in our pain: it is His megaphone to rouse a deaf world."[3]

---

3. Lewis, *Problem of Pain*, 91.

In the nineties, I listened to a lament sung by Mary Achol Deng in the killing fields of South Sudan. Deng's prayerful cry expressed grief over the loss of her people, describing children slaughtered, communities abandoned, and pastors murdered. She spoke of powerlessness in the face of oppression, pleading for Christ's mercy and strength as her people suffered under unjust laws and violent rulers.[4]

Sadly, our world is far too often deaf to God's megaphone. In my ministry, I have seen firsthand the suffering and pain of the church worldwide. In 1998, I published a book, *Hear My People's Cry*, which detailed the suffering of the South Sudanese people. As I wrote, "We are children of God, created in His image from one essence. Jesus Christ binds us together as 'one body and one spirit.'"[5] Yet, "one Lord, one faith, one baptism, one God and Father of all" (Eph 4:5) is often lost in the world.[6] Instead of hearing God's shout in the pain of others or ourselves, we retreat into our worlds. The South Sudanese people, or Christians in Pakistan, both fellow Christians who share "one faith, one baptism" and are a part of the universal church, have often been forgotten and ignored. Their cry for help—God's megaphone calling us to do something—has fallen on deaf ears.

Let me share a short excerpt of my letter to the president of the United States on behalf of the Pakistan Christian community:

> Dear Mr. President: In your speech to the Muslim world in Cairo on June 4, 2009, you said, "Violent extremists have exploited these tensions in a small but potent minority of Muslims." It is true, and now this "potent minority" is becoming a large majority of extremists conducting violent acts against innocent human beings. In Pakistan, the justification for the attacks on Christians is based on the draconian Blasphemy Law sections 295-B and 295-C passed in the National Assembly in 1982. In its selective application, it has provided a pretext for private vendettas, but its victims almost have been Christians.

4. Deng, "Voice from Sudan."
5. Augustine, *Hear My People's Cry*, 25.
6. Scripture quotation in this chapter is from the KJV.

Suffering Is God's Megaphone

> Religious persecution, wherever it occurs, diminishes us all and demands more than finger-wagging in response. I sincerely pray that God shall use you to bring an end to the persecution of Christians in Pakistan.[7]

Yet, I received no reply. Even the leader of the first world, who had just mentioned in his speech about violent extremism in Cairo, was deaf to the suffering of God's people in Pakistan. Suffering is not something that is restricted to Pakistani Christian and South Sudanese refugee camps or persecuted Christians around the globe. Lewis draws on his own lived experiences to highlight his journey, a journey filled with suffering. In *Surprised by Joy*, the semi-autobiographical book about his childhood and life after his conversion to Christianity, Lewis describes an idyllic early childhood. Yet, it was lonely, and then it was shattered by a series of traumatic events that ultimately contributed to his loss of faith as a young man. As is fitting for the future prolific author, Lewis's describes his early childhood:

> I am a product of long corridors, empty sunlit rooms, upstairs indoor silences, attics explored in solitude, distant noises of gurgling cisterns and pipes, and the noise of wind under the tiles. Also, of endless books. My father bought all the books he read and never got rid of any of them. There were books in the study, books in the drawing room, books in the cloakroom, books (two deep) in the great bookcase on the landing, books in a bedroom, books piled as high as shoulder in the cistern attic, books of all kinds reflecting every transient state of my parents' interests, books readable and unreadable, books suitable for a child and books most emphatically not. Nothing was forbidden to me. In the seemingly endless rainy afternoons, I took volume after volume from the shelves. I always had the certainty of finding a book that was new to me as a man who walks into a field has of finding a new blade of grass.[8]

---

7. Augustine, "Letter."
8. Lewis, *Surprised by Joy* (1955), 9–10.

Alongside Lewis's life of books, he described

> good parents, good food, and a garden (which seemed large) to play in. I began life with two other blessings. One was our nurse, Lizzie Endicott, in whom even the exacting childhood memory can discover no flaw—nothing but kindness, gaiety, and good sense. Lizzie was, as nearly as a human can be, simply good... The other blessing was my brother. Though three years my senior, he never seemed to be an elder brother; we were allies.[9]

Supported in a healthy and loving, though lonely, environment, religion was a secondary element of Lewis's childhood. Although his mother's father was an Anglican Church of Ireland rector, religion seemed to play a minor role in Lewis's early childhood. *Surprised by Joy* makes few references to religion in Lewis's early childhood. Instead, Lewis focused on the pleasures of his brother's companionship and the imaginative world they created.

However, this paradise ended abruptly with his mother's death. Flora Lewis was only forty-six when cancer claimed her life. C. S. was only nine, and his mother's death was a shock to the entire family. As Lewis wrote, "With my mother's death all settled happiness, all that was tranquil and reliable, disappeared from my life. There was to be much fun, many pleasures, many stabs of Joy; but no more of the old security. It was sea and islands now; the great continent had sunk like Atlantis."[10]

Jack and his brother Warnie's misery was compounded by their father's disastrous decision to place the boys in a brutal boarding school in Surrey, England. Wynyard, the boarding school, was run by a vicious headmaster, Robert Capron, known as "Oldie" to the boys. Capron was an unstable individual who was sadistic, cruel, and arbitrary. Wynyard was a nightmarish place. The school had one classroom, no library, no laboratories, and no athletic field. An enduring memory of the school was the stench of the outdoor toilets that "even in 1905 any Sanitary Inspector

---

9. Lewis, *Surprised by Joy* (1955), 4.
10. Lewis. *Surprised by Joy* (1955), 23.

would have unhesitatingly condemned."[11] C. S. Lewis later called the school Belsen after the Nazi concentration camp. The Lewis brothers endured Wynyard for two years until the school was closed after another student brought a court action against Capron's abuses. Ultimately, Oldie was committed to an insane asylum, and the school never reopened.

Wynyard also gave Lewis an early and lingering distrust and distaste for religion. Students were required to attend Anglo-Catholic services twice on Sunday. A diary entry from 1909 makes it clear that young Lewis's early impressions were highly negative: "We were obliged to go to St John's, a church which wanted to be Roman Catholic, but was afraid to say so. A kind of church abhorred by respectful Irish Protestants . . . In this abominable place of Romish hypocrites and English liars, the people cross themselves, bow to the Lord's Table . . . and pray to the Virgin."[12]

For the young Lewis, such spiritual experience and faith were unsurprisingly, not exhilarating but oppressive, and it seems the serious beliefs of Wynyard did not long outlast his stay there. It was an experience of a joyless and legalistic faith. The God he envisioned was one of anger and wrath. As Downing put it, "The lonely little boy imprisoned himself in a religion of guilt, not grace."[13] He carried a negative image of the church and its place in his life:

> But though I liked clergymen as I liked bears, I had as little wish to be in Church as in the zoo. It was, to begin with, a kind of collective; a wearisome "get-together affair." I couldn't yet see how a concern of that sort should have anything to do with one's spiritual life. To me, religion ought to have been a matter of good men praying alone and meeting by twos and threes to talk of spiritual matters.[14]

Here, Lewis draws a picture of a spiritually dry, boring, and lifeless church. It utters and mutters mechanical worship. Services lack joy

---

11. Downing, *Most Reluctant Convert*, 36.
12. Downing, *Most Reluctant Convert*, 40–41.
13. Downing, *Most Reluctant Convert*, 44.
14. Lewis, *Surprised by Joy* (1955), 286.

and life-giving spirituality. This church fails to energize the community to be on the mission of Christ. Lewis's brother refers to the "dry husks of religion offered by the semi-political churchgoing of Ulsters."[15] Os Guinness describes how the "Christian church too often abandoned its Biblical calling and became the chaplain to the status quo and even the cheerleader to a series of oppressive establishments."[16]

In the third millennium, the church is in a dry season. We are losing members in mainline churches. Yet, at this time, C. S. Lewis gives us hope. C. S. Lewis wrote most of his works from the 1930s through the early 1960s, arguing against modernism and postmodernism's attempt to reject the sacred and elevate the secular.[17] C. S. Lewis reminds us that the church must focus on our original call. As a resurrection community, we must talk about life in the face of death—because Jesus' charge to the church is to be *ecclesia*, which is from the Greek verb *eccaleo*, meaning to call out or summon forth.

> Go therefore and make all the nations my disciples [disciple all the nations], baptizing them [i.e., all the nations] in the name of the Father and of the Son and of the Holy Spirit, teaching them [i.e., all the nations] to observe all things that I have commanded you. (Matt 28:18–20)

In the third millennium, Lewis reminds us that we have two options. "Either we will build Gothic cathedrals again, from a restored faith, or we will build the Tower of Babel again, from a restored apostasy."[18]

Jesus sends the apostles to proclaim the kingdom (Matt 10). In doing so, we live out the charge of the gospel by word and action to promote nothing but the common good: healing the sick, raising the dead, cleansing lepers, casting out demons, and standing on the side of the downtrodden and outcasts for justice and dignity

---

15. Schakel, *Large Enough*, 140.
16. Guinness, *Magna Carta of Humanity*, 12.
17. Muehlenberg, Review, para. 3.
18. Peter Kreeft, in Muehlenberg, Review, para. 10.

of every human being. This vibrant, living church is opposite of the rigid conformity and emptiness that Lewis experienced in his early church experiences—the legalistic and conforming church. Instead, the church is never meant to be purposeless and boring but filled with action and guided by the gospel manifesto to be in the public square. The church is sensitive to the pain and suffering of persecution, COVID lockdowns, racism, Black Lives Matter, and the "Me Too" movement. The community of Jesus feels the pain of our actions that cause damage to the creative order. We need to participate to redeem our planet Earth's suffering because we humans have caused such havoc in the pollution of God's wonderful creation. Maltbie Babcock's beloved hymn "This Is My Father's World," based on Ps 89:11, can become our gospel theme song to save our planet:

> This is my Father's world:
> O let me ne'er forget
> That though the wrong seem oft so strong,
> God is the Ruler yet.
> This is my Father's world:
> Why should my heart be sad?
> The Lord is King: let the heavens ring!
> God reigns; let earth be glad![19]

The Christian faith invites us to come out into the world and be involved where humanity is in pain and experiences suffering of many kinds. C. S. Lewis in *A Grief Observed* gives readers permission to feel and express their anger, confusion, doubts, and resentments—permitted by the fact that Lewis experienced them himself. He now recognizes them as part of the process of encountering grief or pain. Lewis slowly and gradually learns to surrender himself more fully to God through his experience of suffering; it shows how his faith is rebuilt and strengthened through what he has endured. As Job says to his friends, "Though he slay me, yet will I trust in him" (Job 13:15).

Lewis's later works in many ways, and his understanding of God is a response to the suffering and traumatic experience that

---

19. Babcock, "This Is My Father's World," st. 3.

began at Wynyard. For all its horror, Wynyard gave Lewis an acute understanding of suffering and, equally important, the idea of God and religion as an oppressive burden. In *The Pilgrim's Regress*, Lewis describes the feeling of leaving this God. Lewis describes the feeling of leaving this God as one of relief, as if a significant burden of guilt, recrimination, and fear had been relieved.[20] Here, the character John is liberated by losing his faith and putting aside the black hole that threatens and accuses him of making mistakes. In *The Pilgrim's Regress*, Lewis articulates a version of religion that is far too common—religion as a source of oppression.

In *The Problem of Pain*, pain can serve as God's megaphone to rouse a deaf world in a positive sense. Pain in *The Pilgrim's Regress*'s megaphone calls attention to our failures, inadequacies, and continual sins. These feelings form the black hole from which John, the *Pilgrim's Regress*'s main character, is relieved to escape.

A part of Lewis's enduring appeal is these candid discussions of all facets of religion. He speaks the language of the unbelievers and the doubters because he was one himself. His doubts and atheism matured from his initial revulsion at Wynyard through his growth as a thinker. He studied under an old-fashioned, free-thinking atheist tutor who fostered Lewis's studies in logic and reasoning. At another school, he had a kind matron who took the Lewis brothers under her care. She, too, had rejected organized, conforming Christianity and embraced spiritualism. In *Surprised by Joy*, Lewis recalls that his materialistic "faith" began to waver toward the end of his stay with Kirkpatrick. In reading literary figures with occult interests, such as William Butler Yeats and Maurice Meterlinck, he began to contemplate the great "perhaps," the possibility that there might be a great deal going on in the universe not readily accessible to the senses. His occult speculations swayed him in a different direction, serving to insulate him against the Christian faith. Every few months, this tension would become so great that he allowed himself a brief "magical excursion," some

---

20. Downing, *Most Reluctant Convert*, 46–47. See Lewis, *Pilgrim's Regress*, 14.

reading or experiment, "in the spookical direction."[21] All of this occult exploration gave him feelings of excitement, then fears of dark forces of ghosts and bogeys.

Lewis's interest in magic and occultism cooled down when, in his twenties, he met magicians and occultists while he was at Oxford. One example is his friend Dr. John Askins, who developed a great interest in the practice of spiritualism, seances, and the occult. Lewis watched his complete psychic collapse, and Askins died in his mid-forties. Downing writes, "In later years, Lewis found a great deal of philosophical significance in his youthful flirtation with what he called magic. But the immediate effect was a sense that spiritual realities were less remote, less hypothetical than he had previously believed. Good and evil began to seem less philosophical postulates than unseen spiritual forces. Later, Lewis did not say his youthful interest in the occult was dangerous or deceptive; he says more emphatically that it was a stratagem of "the enemy."[22]

It took several decades and joining the Oxford English faculty before Lewis embraced Christianity. In 1929, Lewis, a hard-boiled atheist at the time, began teaching at Oxford, where he befriended two Christians. They were H. V. D. Dyson and J. R. R. Tolkien. He was increasingly attracted to reading Christian authors, especially Samuel Johnson, George MacDonald, and G. K. Chesterton. He describes in his memoir *Surprised by Joy* his two conversion experiences:

> [friendship with Tolkien] marked the breakdown of two old prejudices. At my first coming into the world I had been (implicitly) warned never to trust a Papist, and at my first coming into the English Faculty (explicitly) never to trust a philologist. Tolkien was both.[23]

Meeting Tolkien and other Christian members of the Oxford community marked the beginning of Lewis's conversion. Even in his

---

21. Downing, *Most Reluctant Convert*, 101–2.
22. Downing, *Into the Region of Awe*, 41.
23. Lewis, *Surprised by Joy* (1955), 264.

most fervent atheist period, Lewis was deeply interested in myths and stories. He pored over a variety of classical and contemporary literature, with a special interest in mythology. And it was through mythology that he took his first steps towards Christianity.

> On September 19, 1931, in what might rank as one of the most critical conversations in literary history, Lewis took his friend and colleague J. R. R. Tolkien on a walk along the River Cherwell near Magdalen College. . . .
>
> As Lewis recounted the conversation in his autobiography, *Surprised by Joy*, Tolkien insisted that myths were not falsehoods but intimations of a concrete, spiritual reality. "Jack, when you meet a god sacrificing himself in a pagan story, you like it very much. You are mysteriously moved by it," Tolkien said. Lewis agreed: Tales of sacrifice and heroism stirred up within him a sense of longing—but not when he encountered them in the gospels.
>
> The pagan stories, Tolkien insisted, are God expressing himself through the minds of poets: They are "splintered fragments" of a much greater story. The account of Christ and his death and resurrection is a kind of myth, he explained. It works on our imagination in much the same way as other myths, with this difference: It really happened.[24]

Perhaps only Tolkien, with his immense intelligence and creativity, could have persuaded Lewis that his reason and imagination might become allies in the act of faith.

Over the next two years Lewis started opening his heart to seek inner peace and to address his longing for joy. He questioned and talked with Tolkien and other Christians. Reluctantly, he began by kneeling and soon found himself praying. He also pored over a variety of classical and contemporary writings, seeking ideas and answers. Of all the texts Lewis read during his spiritual apprenticeship, the one that affected him the most was the Gospel of John (in Greek), which he said made all other religious writings seem like a comedown. As Lewis wrote:

24. Loconte, "How Lewis Accepted Christianity," paras. 6–8.

Suffering Is God's Megaphone

> I was by now too experienced in literary criticism to regard the Gospels as myths. They had not the mythical taste. And yet the very matter which they set down in their artless, historical fashion—those narrow, unattractive Jews, too blind to the mythical wealth of the Pagan world around them—was precisely the matter of great myths. If ever a myth had become fact, had been incarnated, it would be just like this . . . Myths were like it in one way. Histories were like it in another. But nothing was simply like it . . . Here and here only in all time the myth must have become fact; the Word, flesh; God, Man. This is not "a religion," nor "a philosophy." It is the summing up and actuality of them all . . . To accept Incarnation was a further step in the same direction. It brings God nearer, or near in a new way. And this, I found was something I had not wanted.[25]

Gradually, Lewis moved towards Christianity. In his own words, Christianity was not something that he had wanted to find when he embarked on his spiritual journey. Yet, inexorably, his beliefs and ideas were shifting and pulling him towards that very place he did not want to go. First, he renounced atheism and accepted that there may be a god behind everything. Theism appealed to Lewis; it provided the idea of a god without the damaging baggage of the joyless and legalistic Christianity he had experienced. Yet, as appealing as theism may have been, it failed to satisfy Lewis's deeper spiritual longings. Finally, reluctant Lewis made the final step and accepted Christianity. As he wrote:

> You must picture me alone in that room in Magdalen, night after night, feeling, whenever my mind lifted even for a second from my work, the steady, unrelenting approach of Him whom I so earnestly desired not to meet. That which I greatly feared had at last come upon me. In the Trinity Term of 1929 I gave in, and admitted that God was God, and knelt and prayed: perhaps, that night, the most dejected and reluctant convert in all England. I did not then see what is now the most shining and obvious thing; the Divine humility which will accept a

---

25. Lewis, *Surprised by Joy* (1955), 288–89.

convert even on such terms. The Prodigal Son at least walked home on his own feet. But who can duly adore that Love which will open the high gates to a prodigal who is brought in kicking, struggling, resentful, and darting his eyes in every direction for a chance of escape? The words *compelle intrare*, compel them to come in, have been so abused by wicked men that we shudder at them; but, properly understood, they plumb the depth of the Divine mercy. The hardness of God is kinder than the softness of men, and His compulsion is our liberation.[26]

Importantly, Lewis did not attempt to equate liberation with an ending of pain and suffering. Instead, he explored the difficult question of why a good and powerful God allows for evil. Evil which causes suffering and pain. As someone who had experienced suffering and spiritual emptiness, Lewis argued that God uses suffering for a purpose—to make us better competent. In the novel *The Horse and His Boy*, Aslan, the Christlike lion, transforms into a much less majestic and more comforting cat to soothe Shasta, the main character. This is summed up on the cross of Christ:

> [Christ], though he was in the form of God[,] did not regard equality with God as something to be exploited, but emptied himself, taking the form of a slave, being born in human likeness. And being found in human form, he humbled himself, and became obedient to the point of death—even death on a cross. (Phil 2:6–8)

And in John 3:16, "For God so loved the world that he gave his Only son so that everyone who believes in him may not perish but may have eternal life." Lewis's definition of love "is not an affectionate feeling, but a steady wish for the loved person's ultimate good as far as it can be obtained."[27] Lewis reminds us of the importance of love, the supreme answer to the pain and suffering caused by evil, which led Christ to the cross. Lewis's most cited verse was "My God, my God, why hast thou forsaken me? The crucifixion cannot be neatly summarized as something moral—in fact, the

---

26. Lewis, *Surprised by Joy* (1955), 279–80.
27. As quoted in Cootsona, *C. S. Lewis and the Crisis*, 129.

travesty of justice that brought Jesus to the cross is profoundly immoral. Only God could use the immorality of evil to develop our moral character . . . or to shape our souls. In other words, evil is how God can develop and transform us."[28]

In my ministry among oppressed communities in Sudan and Pakistan, I have been an eyewitness to the horrible destruction and pain of human beings. In February 1996, while visiting Kakuma Refugee Camp in Kenya, I heard Bishop Nathaniel Garang, bishop of Bor, South Sudan, preaching on Sunday morning: "This Kakuma is the school of God. Here is the place where we find God. Even though we are suffering, God is with us." We flew further into Bor, Sudan's war zone area, where more than a million were killed and hundreds of thousands displaced. I witnessed the suffering of the persecuted community and their triumphant living faith in their songs while lifting high wooden Dinka crosses and singing a hymn that expresses a heartfelt plea for God's peace amid continual affliction and the pain of humanity, acknowledging the world's persistent hardships and the sighs of souls yearning for eternal life. It calls for a firm grasp of the cross as a symbol of salvation and steadfast hope while waiting for the promise of eternal life to unfold. The hymn concludes with a strong personal declaration of unwavering faith in Jesus as the only way and source of salvation, reflecting the resilience, hope, and deep devotion of a community enduring suffering through steadfast trust in God.

I wrote in my journal following thoughts that night:

> The Living faith of the persecuted church has grown from the cross of Christ. The cross has become their proud symbol of the strength to live and die for Jesus Christ. The followers of Jesus in this land of oppression and killing fields have adopted the cross to symbolize the only life they want to live. In the sign of the cross, they conquer the forces of darkness, oppression, hatred and evil. To them, the cross represents their daily struggle, the pain of betrayal, suffering, affliction and the triumphant faith to follow Christ. "For the message about the

---

28. Cootsona, *C. S. Lewis and the Crisis*, 129.

cross is foolishness to those who are perishing, but to us who are being saved it is the power of God" (1 Cor 1:17).[29]

On January 29, 2023, days before a historic visit to South Sudan with Pope Francis and the Rt Rev. Dr. Iain Greenshields, moderator of the Scottish Presbyterian Church, Archbishop of Canterbury Justin Welby issued a statement:

> Our visit is a Pilgrimage of Peace. We come as servants—to listen to and amplify the cries of the South Sudanese people, who have suffered so much and continue to suffer because of conflict, devast[at]ing flooding, widespread famine and much more. Over the past three years and even since July, violence has intensified in many parts of the country. We hope to review and renew the commitments made by South Sudanese leadership at the Vatican in 2019, and the commitments they have made to their people since then.
>
> We come as brothers in Christ to worship together and witness to the God who reconciles us. The communities of South Sudan have a legacy of powerful witness to their faith. Through working together, they have been a sign and instrument of the reconciliation God desires for their whole country and all of creation. We hope to build on and reenergise that legacy.
>
> This will be a historic visit. After centuries of division, leaders of three different parts of the Church are coming together in an unprecedented way, and in so doing are seeking to be part of answering another prayer—Jesus' prayer—that his followers might be one—"ut unum sint" (John: 17). We come as followers of Jesus, the Prince of Peace, knowing that his Holy Spirit is at work in South Sudan and has the power to transform hearts. His love and welcome are on offer to all. It is through him that we find our deepest peace and our most profound hopes for

---

29. Augustine, *Hear*, 28.

justice. And so I ask you to pray with us for the people of South Sudan.[30]

Jesus spoke of suffering as being "for God's glory" so that God's Son might be glorified, thus completing the work of salvation through his sacrifice on the cross. Lewis also spoke of pain as the megaphone God will use to rouse a deaf world. In the case of persecuted churches, pain and suffering brought them close to God, making them the fastest-growing churches. Our experience tells us that God's megaphone can make some followers deaf, but not all.

This vision of suffering as the path to glory for the people of God is undoubtedly biblical. However, one cannot say the same for attempts to universalize the principle and apply it to all suffering without exception. True, Jesus referred to wars, earthquakes, and famines as the beginning of birth pains heralding the emergence of the new world (Mark 13:8). Paul similarly likened nature's frustration, bondage to decay, and groans to "the pains of childbirth" (Rom 8:22). But these are references to the apocalyptic promise of renewal for both society and nature; they are not applied in the Bible to the salvation of individuals or peoples.[31] Meanwhile, within the community of those whom God in mercy has redeemed, it should be possible for us to echo Paul's affirmation that "we also rejoice in our sufferings" because "we rejoice in the hope of the glory of God" (Rom 5:2–3).

Joni Eareckson Tada, a promising athlete who was only seventeen when she was paralyzed in a diving accident in the Chesapeake Bay, was left a total quadriplegic, paralyzed from the neck down. In her personal testimony she describes how she was full of pain, frustration, resentment, and even suicidal depression. She was angry at God. Her family and community of faith stayed with her during this dark period of her deep suffering. She saw a vision of Jesus on the cross, immobilized, paralyzed, and equally as helpless as she was. In that vision, she also saw the resurrected Christ. She wrote, "I have hope for the future now. The Bible speaks of our

---

30. Archbishop of Canterbury, "Archbishop Calls for Prayer," paras. 10–12.
31. Stott, *Cross of Christ*, 324–25.

bodies being 'glorified' in heaven. I now know the meaning of being 'glorified.' In time, after my death, I'll be on my feet dancing."[32] She said, "I can scarcely believe it. I—with shriveled, bent fingers, atrophied muscles, gnarled knees and no feeling from the shoulders down—will one day have a new body, light, bright and clothed in righteousness, powerful and dazzling. No other religion, no other philosophy promises new bodies, hearts, and minds. Only in the Gospel of Christ do hurting people find such incredible hope."[33] This reflection of her faith is not a mere comforting idea for her. It is an authentic revelation of Christ's faithful promise not to leave us alone but to always be with us. Suffering can lead us to cling to God. "I will not leave you as orphans; I will come to you" (John 14:18). Lewis's favorite verse in the Bible was Jesus' cry of dereliction, "My God, my God, why have you forsaken me?" According to Lewis, this turning to God in suffering remains so central to our growth that the devil shudders. In his advice to the junior tempter Wormwood, the senior tempter Screwtape warns of a particularly dangerous moment for their cause: when someone, though no longer feeling the desire to follow God, still chooses to do what is right even while the world feels empty of any divine presence. This moment—when a person feels abandoned yet continues to obey—poses a serious challenge to temptation, because their will stays committed to goodness despite the lack of comfort or clear signs of God's nearness. It is precisely in this perseverance, through spiritual dryness and doubt, that the resolve to follow God's will is most powerfully tested—and most threatening to the forces of evil.[34]

Lewis had significant periods in which he suffered and experienced pain (i.e., the death of his mother in 1908, his father's distance, his traumatic boyhood, and his experiences in the boarding schools.) He experienced the horrors of war in World War I. He lived with his dear brother Warnie's alcoholism, which led to his brother's many hospitalizations. His middle life was his long-term commitment to take care of Janie Moore's declining health,

---

32. Yancey, *Where Is God*, 120.
33. Tada, *Heaven*, 53.
34. Lewis, *Screwtape Letters*, 47.

and she was a complex woman whose demands caused Lewis great suffering. Later in life, he experienced the death of his beloved wife, Joy. Joy's death stirred a profound pain and confronted him as all human beings felt its punch. So, Lewis had as much right as anyone to examine the "problem of pain." "Man that is born of woman is of few days and full of trouble," and "he comes forth like a flower and is cut down: he flees also as a shadow, and continues not" (Job 14:1–2).

After his whole life of experiencing pain and suffering, Lewis comes to faith in Christ, much like suffering communities of faith in Sudan and Pakistan or as an individual like Joni Eareckson Tada. Lewis goes from being an ardent atheist to "the most reluctant convert" who believed in the redemptive power and saving grace of Jesus Christ. Lewis believed in heaven and thus life after death. If he was right about his writing, his place is now secure. It is undoubtedly better. He understood how God can use suffering for a purpose—to make us better. His lifelong quest for joy through periods of doubt and spiritual emptiness led him to question if there is a good God ("Had God designed the world, it would not be / A world so frail and faulty as we see").[35] Lewis's longing for *Sehnsucht* now led him to the joy of heaven, a place now secure and certainly better. This joy resonates in his movingly in some of the final words from *The Chronicles of Narnia*. The conclusion reflects the idea that all the experiences and adventures in Narnia and in their earthly lives were merely the beginning, like a title page or cover to a much grander, eternal story. This story—unlike any earthly tale—is endlessly unfolding, with each chapter surpassing the last in wonder and significance. Rather than an ending, it marks a glorious beginning to a timeless journey that no one on earth has fully read or comprehended, representing hope, renewal, and infinite progression beyond the confines of ordinary life.[36] In Christ, we can trust God in our times of trials, pain, and suffering and say:

---

35. Lewis, *Surprised by Joy* (2017), 78.
36. See Lewis, *Last Battle*, 180.

> I consider that the sufferings of this present time are not worth comparing with the glory about to be revealed to us. . . . If God is for us, who is against us? Who will separate us from the love of Christ? Will hardship, or distress, or persecution, or famine, or nakedness, or peril, or sword? . . . No, in all these things we are more than conquerors through him who loved us. For I am convinced that neither death, nor life, not angels, nor anything else in all creation, will be able to separate us from the love of God in Christ Jesus our Lord. (Rom 8:18, 31–35, 37–39)

Lewis's "Christian commitment became so complete that Lewis declared without hesitation that pain was 'God's megaphone' to rouse us out of complacency or God's 'chisel' to perfect our form."[37] It is this faith I have personally found in persecuted Christian communities of Sudan and Pakistan. In experiencing pain, suffering, and challenges, they did not give up but lifted high the cross of Jesus to acknowledge:

> I have decided to follow Jesus,
> I have decided to follow Jesus,
> I have decided to follow Jesus,
> No turning back, no turning back.
>
> The world behind me, the cross before me;
> The world behind me, the cross before me;
> The world behind me, the cross before me;
> No turning back, no turning back.[38]

In Sudan and Pakistan, the persecuted Christian communities' new understanding of the pain and suffering of the cross of Jesus Christ is *crux probat Omanis* (the test that proves everything).

---

37. Conn, *C. S. Lewis and Human Suffering*, 11.
38. "I Have Decided," st. 1–2.

Bibliography

Archbishop of Canterbury. "Archbishop Calls for Prayer Ahead of Historic Joint Visit to South Sudan." Archbishop of Canterbury, Jan. 29, 2023. https://www.archbishopofcanterbury.org/news/news-and-statements/archbishop-calls-prayer-ahead-historic-joint-visit-south-sudan.

Augustine, Patrick. *Hear My People's Cry*. Self-published, 1998.

———. "Letter to President Barack H. Obama." Aug. 3, 2009. In the author's possession.

Babcock, Maltbie D. "This Is My Father's World." In *The United Methodist Hymnal*, #144. Nashville: United Methodist, 1989.

Conn, Marie A. *C. S. Lewis and Human Suffering: Light Among the Shadows*. Mahwah, NJ: Hidden Spring, 2008.

Cootsona, Gregory S. *C. S. Lewis and the Crisis of a Christian*. Louisville: Westminster John Knox, 2014.

Deng, Mary Achol. "Poem: A Voice from Sudan." Translated by Marc Nikkel. Kakuma Refugee Camp, Diocese of Bor, Kenya, 1997.

Downing, David C. *Into the Region of Awe: Mysticism in C. S. Lewis*. Downers Grove, IL: Intervarsity, 2005.

———. *The Most Reluctant Convert: C. S. Lewis's Journey to Faith*. Eugene, OR: Wipf & Stock, 2004.

Guinness, Os. *The Magna Carta of Humanity: Sinai's Revolutionary Faith and the Future of Freedom*. Downers Grove, IL: InterVarsity, 2021.

"I Have Decided to Follow Jesus." In *Choice Light and Life Songs: A Collection of the Best Loved Gospel Songs and Choruses, Both Old and New*, edited by LeRoy M. Lowell, #168. Winona Lake, IN: Light and Life, 1950.

Lewis, C. S. *A Grief Observed*. San Francisco: HarperSanFrancisco, 2001.

———. *The Last Battle*. New York: HarperCollins, 1956.

———. *Letters to Malcolm: Chiefly on Prayer*. New York: Harcourt, Brace, and World, 1964.

———. *The Pilgrim's Regress: An Allegorical Apology for Christianity, Reason and Romanticism*. Quebec: Samizdat, 1933.

———. *The Problem of Pain*. New York: Macmillan, 1940.

———. *The Screwtape Letters*. New York: HarperOne, 2001.

———. *Surprised by Joy: The Shape of My Early Life*. New York: Harcourt, Brace, 1955.

———. *Surprised by Joy: The Shape of My Early Life*. San Francisco: HarperOne, 2017.

Loconte, Joseph. "How C. S. Lewis Accepted Christianity." Heritage Foundation, Apr. 5, 2021. https://www.heritage.org/civil-society/commentary/how-c-s-lewis-accepted-christianity.

Muehlenberg, Bill. Review of *C. S. Lewis for the Third Millennium*, by Peter Kreeft. CultureWatch, June 5, 2005. https://billmuehlenberg.com/2005/06/05/a-review-of-cs-lewis-for-the-third-millennium-by-peter-kreeft/.

Schakel, Peter J. *Is Your Lord Large Enough?* Downers Grove, IL: Intervarsity, 2008.

Stott, John R. W. *The Cross of Christ.* Downers Grove, IL: Intervarsity, 1986.

Tada, Joni Eareckson. *Heaven: Your Real Home.* Grand Rapids: Zondervan, 1997.

Turley, K. V. "Remembering C. S. Lewis: A Brief Friendship That Changed a Life." *National Catholic Register*, Nov. 22, 2019. https://www.ncregister.com/interview/remembering-c-s-lewis-a-brief-friendship-that-changed-a-life.

Yancey, Philip. *Where Is God When It Hurts?* Grand Rapids: Zondervan, 2002.

2

Perichoretic Hymnody

Perelandra as Model for Theological Poetics

JUNIUS JOHNSON

THEOLOGICAL POETICS IS A set of practices that has great potential for supporting and expanding the work of philosophical theology. This is always true, but it is especially so in the current cultural moment when many non-theologians need a compelling invitation to engage with the more involved discussions of philosophical theology. To deploy this tool effectively, we need to understand what it is and what it is good for, and how to practice it. C. S. Lewis offers us just the model we need for theological poetics in the second book of his *Cosmic Trilogy*, *Perelandra*.

In the last chapter of that work, five characters engage in a rhapsodic hymn in praise of what they call "the Great Dance," which refers to all of creation. The defining characteristic of this dance is a mutual ceding to other elements in the dance that renders it a clear image of *perichoresis*, the circle dance that is often applied to the persons of the Trinity. Thus, the hymn at the culmination of *Perelandra* is directly linked to a theological locus that grounds and controls the unfolding of that hymn. This makes it a good place to see the dynamics of theological poetics at work.

In what follows, I will explain what I mean by theological poetics and show how the image of perichoresis in *Perelandra* is an example of the deployment of theological poetics. I will conclude by tracing some of the payoffs of this approach.

What Is Theological Poetics?

First off, what is poetics? Usually, the term means the principles that guide the composition and analysis of literature. That may be overly formal, but it can work if only we are willing to broaden our understanding of the word "principle."

I would take the relevant principles not to be anything discursive in the first instance. This rules out literary techniques as readily as it rules out philosophical suppositions. Both are tools that may be deployed in the service of poetics, but they are not its principles. Instead, the principles are what I would call poetic vision.

Poetic vision describes a peculiar (and therefore unique) way of viewing the world. It expresses that a particular person sees the world in a certain way. It is the very *this-ness* of reflective experience. It must be reflective: not just any vision, but a poetic vision. *Poiesis* is making, and so there has to be the deployment of *ars* in the broadest sense: a skill applied to bring order, to synthesize or systematize. Many of those words may feel too stuffy for a concept so lofty as poetic vision, but so long as they are not taken in the sense of their rationalistic abuse, they will serve very well for the purpose. Poetic vision both begins in and aims at an intuition of the whole. Gestalt is as indispensable to poetic vision as it is to systematic theology; the type of whole that will satisfy us is different in the two instances.

The ars poetica need not be the formal arts of the poetry schools, however. It does not take formal training to organize intuitions into Gestalten; however, much formal training may greatly benefit the task. Indeed, insofar as the poetic vision does its first work at the level of intuition, every poetic vision first arises in the world of experience, and some then go on to be honed by formal training. And so the training as such is external to the task of seeing poetically. This does not amount to the democratization of poetic vision but rather the de-elitizing of it. The capacity for poetic vision is the common inheritance of humanity, but the power to be a great poet is rarer and more elusive.

Particularity is an irreducible aspect of vision: vision is always someone's vision, and every act of seeing is modulated by the perceptual powers that give rise to it and by the conceptual space into which the image is received. And yet my seeing and your seeing are both called "seeing" because of the common faculty and the common process. We both have eyes, but my eyes are not your eyes; they are configured differently in countless ways, and so we do not perceive the same. And my mind is not your mind, shaped as it is by my experiences and choices, and so the interpretive part of vision proceeds differently for me than for you. Likewise, Milton and Dante, for all that they have in common in terms of commitments, influences, and subject matter, see the world and God (that is to say, everything) differently. Each of their visions is Christian, but each is also personal, and persons are non-substitutable, non-repeatable, and non-interchangeable. Neither is definitive, for nothing in the world of creatures is definitive: that is not a property of creatures but is proper to God alone. And so, they see in their characteristic ways and form two different and indispensable poetic visions.

If poetic visions form the principles for poetics, then poetics turns out to be the art of adequating those visions to particular forms and contents, the deployment of appropriate structures to give those visions space to breathe, and the assessing of the congruity of concrete artistic impositions to the vision that is to be expressed through them. Poetics is, in a word, the wisdom of making.

Theological poetics is not merely poetics done with an eye to theological truths. In such an approach, theology remains purely external to the poetic as such. It is no more than a bias or a desideratum that imposes certain limitations on the ways in which the poetic will be exercised and the paths it is allowed to follow. Such a poetics is not theological; it is merely under the thumb of theology, which serves to limit rather than expand it. To meaningfully modify the concept of poetics with an adjective (whether that be Marxist, philosophical, theological, or what have you) is to claim that the adjective fundamentally changes the nature of the poetic. It can be expected that these changes will be fruitful: new insights, connections, and syntheses will come from the fact that the poetics have been modulated in this or that way. The point of specifying poetics is to make it more fecund.

Therefore, a truly theological poetics would have to be one that is theological in its very inner logic, in the structure of how it reasons, in what it takes to be the beautiful, and in how it witnesses to that beauty. Theological poetics is a wisdom of making that is grounded in the vision of the world as being the sort of place it is described as being in theology. It is not simply to treat of the topics of theology in a poetic way, or to employ theological modes in making (and so no number of *Fausts* will make Goethe's vision theological); it is to think the world through the categories of theology and, therefore, to have a poetic vision that is fundamentally shaped by the form of the divine revelation and economy. Christian theological poetics radiates from the vision of Christ as the unsurpassable end of the works of God.

This will not mean that every practitioner of theological poetics will have the same aesthetic tastes or even values, for the point of the unrepeatable specificity of individuality is to ground a symphonic witness to the One God. Accordingly, there will not be a single theopoetics but a panoply, for wisdom is proved true in all her children. But because there is one God and Original Beauty to which all these disparate voices witness, there will nevertheless be an agreement among all those engaged in the task of Christian poetics concerning just what it is that guides the poetic vision. There will be boundaries to this art, such that not just anything whatsoever can claim to be theopoetics.

This will give rise to unexpected rapprochements and intersections that cannot be spelled out ahead of time because they arise from the encounter of two spontaneous and infinitely generative encounters with the ground of all beauty. My encounter with the beauty of God, which grounds and shapes the poetics of my writing, emerges from the depths of my being: how I am made, what I have made of myself, what I am called to be, and the bitter path that leads from where I longed to go to where I must be, and the passions, hopes, fears, and longings that make my whole mental space so *me*; these are finite in extent but infinite in horizon, because pointed at God and able to find fulfillment only in God. And yet they are infinitely generative, for my spontaneity is a created image of the divine omnipotence, the power to bring forth ex nihilo. This is fundamental to what it means to be a person: to be an infinite well of newness, such that no matter how well you know me, I can always surprise you. This creaturely immensity meets a like immensity when it encounters your poetic vision, and both immensities are constantly in motion, ever seeing the world and God anew and changing to adapt to the new horizons of wonder thus revealed. And of course, since these are *theological* poetics, the object of our ultimate intentions is God, who is both infinite in the way all persons are (and, indeed, triply-infinite), but who is also qualitatively infinite, not subject to the limitations of creatureliness, and so always transcendent and transcending of the horizon of creaturely experience. In other words, every aspect of the encounter of two different theopoetics is in motion from an uncapturable past to an unforeseeable (for creatures) future. So much of the fruit of such encounters lies beyond what we could predict.

To be theological, then, a poetics would have to be such that it could not survive the excision of the theological element. The structure would collapse, and be in no meaningful way what it was before. To be sure, a poetics might remain: but it would be as different from the poetics that came before it as faith is different from optimism.

Perelandra and Theopoetics

What we see in Lewis's *Perelandra* is the application of his theopoetics to science fiction. The results are compelling and can provide a model for theopoetical engagement more broadly. The point could be made from any of Lewis's fiction, but among these *Perelandra* has a special place: it is simultaneously the most theological and least allegorical of all of his fiction.

Allegory, "other speaking," may be taken strictly or broadly. Strictly speaking, allegory is one to one: that is to say, everything in the story refers to something else. *The Romance of the Rose*[1] and *Pilgrim's Progress*[2] are like this. There is "other speaking" that is not pedantically one to one. Fables and parables are species of allegory so understood, as is myth.

Typically, in allegory properly speaking one very quickly discards the literal level, or greatly relativizes it. The literal meaning does not need to have the kind of organic cohesion we normally require of stories, because its center is outside of itself: any aspect of the story will be judged to be well or poorly done on the basis of the degree to which it serves the elucidation of the other thing the discourse is about. But in allegory broadly speaking, the literal level must maintain its integrity, because it is not *only* or primarily a vehicle for saying something else, even though it is *fundamentally* a vehicle for saying something else. Like non-allegorical narrative, its center is within itself, even while it is pointed at something beyond itself.

Narnia is allegory in the broad sense, insofar as Lewis himself correlates each of the books to aspects of the Christian life and intentionally recapitulates the major beats of Christian salvation history. It is a supposition, but it is an allegorical supposition.[3]

Till We Have Faces is a myth, and myths have always been allegories.[4] A myth is an allegory meant to explain phenomena in the world. As the original Cupid and Psyche myth allegorizes the relationship of the soul to desire, so Lewis's reworked myth allegorizes the relationship of the soul to the demands of a holy God.

Narnia and *Till We Have Faces* speak more naturally in an allegorical way about our world because they are not our world.

1. Guillaume de Lorris and Jean de Meun, *Romance of the Rose*.
2. Bunyan, *Pilgrim's Progress*.
3. Lewis, *Letters to Children*, 44–45.
4. Lewis, *Till We Have Faces*.

It is not a requirement that the world of the allegory be different from our world; after all, the prophet Nathan tells David an allegory about a man and a sheep as a way of condemning David's relationship to Bathsheba, and men and sheep certainly belong to our world (2 Sam 12). Nevertheless, casting the action in another world creates additional space that makes it easier for the story to *also* be speaking about our world in a broadly allegorical sense.

But *Perelandra* is not an allegory. The planet Perelandra *is* our world. Uncle Andrew makes the distinction clear in *The Magician's Nephew*, where he says that other planets are part of our world because you could reach them by natural means, if you could develop the proper means. What makes something a different world, he argues, is that it is someplace you could never get to by traveling through conventional space and means. There is a discontinuity, and a very different type of travel would be required to get there (such as magic).[5] So even though there is an England in the Narnia books that is ostensibly the same England we could travel to in our world, the stories take place in Narnia, which is another world in Uncle Andrew's sense. Even though we have not been to Mars and can prove that it is not the Malacandra of *Out of the Silent Planet*, nevertheless, internal to the story, it and Perelandra are places that are reached by traveling within our world (using science, not magic), and so are part of our world.

This does not prove that Perelandra is not an allegory; but it would speak less naturally in an allegorical way because of its putative identity with the world we live in. Maleldil is not a supposition like Aslan is; he is not an imagination of what Christ might be like if he were to be instantiated in a different world. Maleldil *is* our Christ, the very one who became incarnate, in what the eldila of the *Cosmic Trilogy* call "strange counsel."[6] As such, it comments on our world not allegorically but directly. It is a theological exploration, more akin to a thought experiment than to a parable. The theological rules that ground it are the same ones that ground the world we live in.

5. See Lewis, *Magician's Nephew*, 23–24.
6. Lewis, *Out of the Silent Planet*, 108.

Given all that has been said, it should be clear that the theopoetical task in writing *Perelandra* is the adequation of the particularities of Lewis's vision of the world suspended in the grace and love of God to a science fiction setting. There are a variety of commitments that Lewis carries over into this fictional world that become, as it were, rules for imagining in this world. Some of these are:

1. The incarnation of Christ is not just historically decisive, it is cosmically decisive.
2. God's creative work is progressive and proceeds to this very day.
3. Something like angels and demons are very active in the created world.
4. Sin is not just an internal inclination; it is something that is urged upon us by our external world.

Each of these becomes a guiding consideration for concrete choices made about the characters, setting, and plot. But they are not sectioned off from one another: there is an interpenetration of these considerations, a clustering around various aspects of the story.

Thus, for example, when Ransom arrives on *Perelandra*, he discovers that the rational creatures (*hnau*) there are humans. This was not how it was on Malacandra, where there were three species of *hnau* as different from one another as they were from humanity. Before Christ had become a creature, there were many possible ways for *hnau* to image him. But the cosmic nature of the incarnation means that from now on, the possible forms have been constrained: not just to humanoid forms, but to actual humans. And so the *hnau* on Perelandra must take human form (commitment 1).[7]

But this is due also to the progressive nature of God's creative work (commitment 2). Though Malacandra, Perelandra, and Thulcandra (Earth) likely formed as planets around the same time

---

7. Lewis, *Perelandra*, 198.

in Lewis's fictional setting, they developed at very different rates. Civilization was already thriving on Malacandra when Adam and Eve came to be on Thulcandra, and it is only in the twentieth century after the incarnation that *hnau* appear on Perelandra. It is the fact that it underwent a different and longer path of development that governs the necessity that, when its *hnau* at last came forth, they would have to be human. Were creation not progressive, or were they to have come about 2500 Earth years sooner, they could have taken another form.

In the gap between when *hnau* appeared on Malacandra and when they appeared on Perelandra (the earliest and latest *hnau* we know about in the trilogy), the celestial being (eldil) responsible for Perelandra was shepherding and nourishing the planet and its life, bringing it to the point where it could bring forth *hnau* (commitment 3).[8] It was part of the means by which the progressive creation of Perelandran *hnau*, which must now be human in form, is accomplished. And because Ransom takes less occasion to sin from the sinfulness of the world around him (commitment 4), he is able to converse with the woman in perfect mutual nudity without the least shadow of sexual longing.[9]

The layering of these commitments and their interaction to produce the story in all of its particulars is evidence of the fact that the theological elements are not accidental to the story's conception or to the poetic in accordance with which the story was produced. Their interaction shows a sort of meta-commitment that informs the poetic at the deepest levels: perichoresis.

Theologically speaking, this is a Trinitarian feature. Whether Lewis came at it through the theologians of the Orthodox tradition or through another path, it is a Trinitarian theme for him as well. From the doctrine of the Trinity, Lewis learned about a kind of distinction in unity that he had seen gestured towards in the myths he so loved, but that could not be resolved within the bounds of the rationalistic philosophy in which he was trained (and of which the science of his day could give no least intimation). The logic of

---

8. Lewis, *Perelandra*, 323.

9. Lewis *Perelandra*, 196.

this interpenetration and radical mutuality is woven throughout his fiction and nonfiction works. But it is nowhere more overt or dazzling than at the end of *Perelandra* in the hymn to the Great Dance.

This hymn, both formally and materially, concretizes the overarching commitment to an interpenetrative perichoresis. The formal aspect comes to the fore in the dissolution of the ability to distinguish subject from object, speaker from hearer. Ransom is not only unable to tell whether a human or an eldil is speaking, he is unable to tell even when he himself or another has spoken. Lewis compares it to five trees standing on a hilltop, all blown by the same wind.[10] We are stripped of the knowledge of which of the five characters says which of the following things, and so we are stripped of perspective: the individuality that each could bring from his or her own experiences is suppressed, or rather, superseded. For it is not that perspective is lacking; it is rather that it is *common*. All five have come to a place from which they can view the universe with the same vision. The final image of the wind in the trees makes that clear. For though perhaps the first association at the mention of the wind blowing is of the Spirit that blows where it will (John 3:8) and is the one giver of diverse gifts (1 Cor 12:4), yet the image goes on to indicate trees swaying together under the same wind: you could no more distinguish the rustling of the one from another. They have all come to one hill, one outlook, and from there, they are blown by one spirit into one vision of the workings of God. Even the distinction between angel and human, between celestial and mundane perspective, breaks down here. Humanity has been elevated to the level of the angels (a significant theme of this last chapter) and can speak with them as equals: not just "with them" in the sense of talking to them, but also in the sense of speaking alongside them.

The material aspect of perichoresis is the Great Dance, which is the subject of this hymnodic collective discourse. It is a dance because of the never-ending mutual ceding of every element within it to every other. Malacandra is said to be to Thulcandra as

---

10. Lewis, *Perelandra*, 340.

a circle is to a sphere; and yet Malacandra can say that Thulcandra was created for the sake of Malacandra. The ancient worlds are at the center, and yet the fallen Thulcandra where the Lord prepared for himself a body is the final cause of the ancient worlds, and so it is at the center. And so it goes.[11]

Each element steps forward to take center stage only to bow and step back to make room for the next. And each thing that was central yields its centrality to the next without ceasing to be central, and in so doing is revealed to be central according to yet another facet of its being. And yet it is not true to say that all is center and there is no periphery: that kind of collapse would destroy the dance, because it would render the whole thing static. No, for it to be a dance, there must be this ebb and flow, this advancing and ceding (cession), a ceding that is not directionless but always aimed *at* something (in-cession), something around which it orbits even as that thing orbits around it and mutually cedes in the direction of the first (*circumincession*). It of course, hardly needs to be pointed out that the literal description of this mutual aroundness (*peri-*) is a *dance* (*choresis*), and so what is said metaphorically of the Trinity is made literal in the creation that images it.

Perelandra thus provides us with a practical instance of the working of theopoetics. But it also demonstrates the most valuable aspect of theopoetics in any age, and certainly in our age. Lewis himself named it in speaking of Narnia: it can sneak past watchful dragons.[12] There is an apologetic trajectory of theopoetics that can reach into places where theology as a discipline cannot, and can touch places that theology can also touch, but in ways that theology cannot.

One challenge to faith is plausibility: for under normal circumstances the human mind will only with difficulty assent to what it judges implausible and will in no way assent to what it judges impossible. Yet to many, the doctrines of faith seem implausible at best, and sometimes even impossible. Theopoetics is able to meet this challenge by displaying what the reader will judge to

11. Lewis, *Perelandra*, 341–42.
12. Lewis, "Sometimes Fairy Stories," 37.

be a plausible impossibility. For fiction divorces plausibility from possibility. That which I find in no way plausible in the news I might find exceedingly plausible in Wonderland or Narnia (nothing is more likely!). The relocating of a theological dynamic from our world to a fictional setting by the working of the theopoetical imagination may allow me to see for the first time the plausibility of it. Now, it is true that I do not go immediately from plausibility to possibility. The plausibility of Jewel the unicorn does not lead me to the possibility of Jewel the unicorn in our world. But this is because what makes Jewel plausible in Narnia is a feature that is not common to our world and Narnia. But what if the features were common? I may find the notion that humans are the lords of creation implausible and impossible; but then I see it imaged in the Lady Tinidril of Perelandra, and how, in an unfallen world, she uses this to elevate the animals, possibly all the way to the point of being themselves *hnau* (and why not?). And then I realize that if we apply this to our world, having made the necessary changes, the only change required is the removal of sin: without sin, nothing more would need to be adjusted to render this possible. In that case, I am perhaps prepared to alter my sense of its impossibility: it is impossible *under present conditions*, but not impossible *simpliciter*. In this way theopoetics can work to build bridges to faith.

Theopoetics also has an internal apologetic value, functioning to welcome those who are put off by the precision and technicality of philosophical theology into the mysteries the technical language is meant to facilitate reflection on. We have already seen a good example of this: perichoresis might be a concept that causes people to want to shut down, and there is no shortage of evidence that Trinitarian theology is a field into which the layman steps only with great trepidation and no small amount of urging. And yet the hymn to the Great Dance, which is essentially doing the same thing, does not trigger the intellectual flight response. Rather, presenting the mystery in terms of compelling imagery that promises immediate understanding without offering anything like ultimacy or total comprehension draws the mind into the mysteries *as mysteries*.

The list of theological and philosophical loci that are thus presented in just the last chapter of *Perelandra* is mind-boggling: idolatry and iconology, the nature of beauty, the image of God, the union of the spiritual and the physical, the nature of evil, the powers of unfallen human nature, the value of hierarchy, the nature of wholeness, the nature of spatial dimensionality and its relationships, original intentions and redemption, supralapsarianism, the ability of all creatures to praise God, the dynamics of divine grace, Trinitarian processions, mutual belonging, and philosophy of time. Many of these are speculative topics (and those that are not inherently speculative are here presented in a speculative vein) that the non-theologian would normally steer clear of. However, theopoetics makes them not only accessible but *desirable*. It is easy to come away from that last chapter wanting to know *more*.

I will go one step further and say that it does not only do this for the layperson. Many a theologian, myself among them, has been and may be inspired and illuminated by the results of the theopoetic imagination. Indeed, even theologians are drawn to and adore theopoetics, which underscores a final aspect that must be made clear: that it is a mode of thinking that differs from the one native to theology. It is not the case that theopoetics can say things theology cannot, but it can say them in a way theology cannot, and that is precisely because of the modal difference between the two. Theopoetics has different rules, different criteria for evaluation, and different methods of proceeding. For that reason, not every theologian is capable of writing imaginatively, and not every literary writer is capable of writing theologically.

But the best of either can do both, and Lewis is an example of that. This is because, while theopoetics is discourse in a distinct mode, it is not therefore external to theology: it is a way of doing theology. I ought, then, not to be opposing theopoetics to theology, but rather to philosophical theology. If this is true, then theopoetics provides a suitable front porch to the study of theology generally and philosophical theology more specifically: before one knows how much one likes it, or even how much of it one is prepared to believe, one can encounter it as rich, vibrant, and delightful. In a culture increasingly suspicious of many of the traditional grounding apologetics of the study of theology, theopoetics has offered and remains a resilient entry point.

Bibliography

Bunyan, John. *The Pilgrim's Progress*. Edited by W. R. Owens. Oxford World's Classics. Oxford: Oxford University Press, 2003.

Guillaume de Lorris, and Jean de Meun. *The Romance of the Rose*. Translated by Frances Horgan. Oxford World's Classics. Oxford: Oxford University Press, 2009.

Lewis, C. S. *Letters to Children*. Edited by Lyle W. Dorsett and Marjorie Lamp Mead. New York: Touchstone, 1985.

———. *The Magician's Nephew*. New York: HarperCollins, 1983.

———. *Out of the Silent Planet*. Vol. 1 of *The Cosmic Trilogy*. New York: Scribner, 1938.

———. *Perelandra*. Vol. 2 of *The Cosmic Trilogy*. New York: Scribner, 1943.

———. "Sometimes Fairy Stories May Say Best What's to Be Said." In *Of Other Worlds: Essays and Stories*, 35–38. San Diego: Harcourt Brace, 1966.

———. *Till We Have Faces: A Myth Retold*. New York: Harcourt, 1956.

3

"Joy Silenced Me"

Sarah Coakley's *Thélogie Totale* in C. S. Lewis's Work and Thought

ANDREW LAZO

THIS ESSAY MAKES THE somewhat counterintuitive claim that we do some disservice to Anglican theology if we fail to consider Oxford don and Cambridge professor C. S. Lewis in some very central and important senses among the Anglican theologians of the twentieth century. To do so, in some ways, requires that we examine what we consider "Anglican" and how we define "theologian." In what sense was Lewis "Anglican"? And in what sense was he a "theologian"? To attempt an answer to these questions, this essay makes three moves. First, it briefly looks at Lewis's extensive reading and writing about Anglican theologians on his own and in earlier centuries. Next, it explores Lewis's role in the Church of England, especially in the 1940s and 50s. Finally, it reads Lewis's work broadly and deeply to discover profound examples of several of the methodologies making up Sarah Coakley's *théologie totale*. By seriously considering Coakley's premises in *God, Sexuality, and the Self: An Essay "On the Trinity,"* we can fruitfully discuss and explore how Lewis's work anticipates and embodies many of those ideas. Supporting that claim will make a place not only for

Coakley's groundbreaking work but also invite a rehabilitative look at Lewis, often too hastily dismissed as merely a popular apologist or a juvenile fiction writer. His resonances with many of Coakley's key concepts strongly suggests that Lewis has a still-considerable voice in theological conversation in the English-speaking world.

As an adult convert to Christianity and a literary historian and critic of great note, C. S. Lewis's writing demonstrates a deep reading of many of the Anglican divines. A small sample will represent Lewis's profound engagement with these writers. His enduringly helpful volume in the Oxford History series, *English Literature in the Sixteenth Century, Excluding Drama*, demonstrates this commitment. Lewis insightfully considers Miles Coverdale, Thomas Cranmer, John Donne, John Foxe, Richard Hooker, John Knox, Hugh Latimer, and William Tyndale, among many others.[1] A glance through some of Lewis's literary essays and vast correspondence reveals careful readings and numerous mentions of many of the key figures in Anglican theology, including Lancelot Andrewes, William Law, Jeremy Taylor, Bishop Butler, St. John Henry Newman, F. D. Maurice, and J. C. Ryle. As a scholar of English literature, Lewis wrote to a surprising extent about Anglican theologians and their ideas in many periods.

In addition to his wide-ranging reading of and writing about Anglican theologians, Lewis found a critical context throughout his life in the Church of England. His maternal great-grandfather, the Rt. Rev. Hugh Hamilton, served as a bishop in the Church of Ireland; his grandfather, the Rev. Thomas Hamilton, served as rector of St. Mark's, Dundela, the Lewis family's home parish in Belfast, from its founding in 1878 until 1900, not long after Lewis's birth in 1898. The Lewis family attended the parish throughout Lewis's young life.[2] College chapel and the local parish continued to prove vital to Lewis's spiritual practice immediately after his return to a belief in theism in the summer of 1930, and feeling that

---

1. Lewis, *English Literature*, 736–43.
2. Smith, "Surprised by Belfast," paras. 1, 3, 5.

one ought to "fly one's flag" as an overt sign of faith, Lewis began a lifelong practice of attending Anglican worship.[3]

Lewis's gifts soon attracted the attention of church leadership, leading to him playing several prominent roles. As Alister McGrath notes:

> Even back in the '40s, senior churchmen were beginning to recognize that Lewis was a remarkable lay theologian, able to connect with contemporary culture in ways that seemed to elude the national Church.
>
> Senior churchmen—including the Regius Professor of Divinity at Oxford University, Oliver Chase Quick, and the Archbishop of Canterbury, William Temple—came to regard Lewis and Dorothy L. Sayers as talented lay theologians, able to communicate effectively with British culture.
>
> Although not himself a theologian in the professional sense of the term, Lewis's first honorary degree was a Doctorate of Divinity, awarded by the University of St Andrews, Scotland, in 1946.
>
> Professor Donald M. Baillie, speaking at the award ceremony on behalf of the Faculty of Divinity, declared that Lewis had "succeeded in capturing the attention of many who will not readily listen to professional theologians," and had "arranged a new kind of marriage between theological reflection and poetic imagination."[4]

In 1947, at the invitation of Lord Salisbury, Lewis attended a meeting with the archbishops of Canterbury and York at Lambeth Palace as part of a select group to discuss the future of the Church of England.[5] Clearly, the immense popular success of *The Screwtape Letters* and of his broadcasts on the BBC (which would become *Mere Christianity*) led Anglican leadership eagerly to seek after Lewis as a spokesman and intermediary between the church and the people. This complex position as an intermediary, however, proved costly to Lewis; most scholars point to his role as

---

3. Lewis, *Surprised by Joy*, 285.
4. McGrath, "Lewis's Appeal to the Imagination," paras. 13–16.
5. Green and Hooper, *C. S. Lewis*, 765–66.

a theological popularizer as one of the causes of much scorn in Oxford, with a resultant loss of professional opportunities.[6] Such writing for a popular audience intriguingly parallels Sarah Coakley's efforts to open her work to a larger public.

As a tutor at Magdalen College, Oxford, and later as professor of medieval and Renaissance literature at Cambridge, Lewis was often invited to preach at the university churches, and he counted several friends among the Anglican clergy. In Oxford, the most notable was the Anglican theologian Austin Farrer, a member of the Inklings, the Oxford writing group that included Lewis, J. R. R. Tolkien, Owen Barfield, Charles Williams, and others. Lewis provided a preface to Farrer's *A Faith of Our Own*; Farrer contributed a valedictory essay on Lewis as "A Christian Apologist" to the Festschrift *Light on C. S. Lewis* a few years after his death.[7] While at Cambridge, he also served on the council of the Anglican theological college Westcott House from 1955 to 1959, once delivering an address to its students at the invitation of the principal, Kenneth Carey (later bishop of Edinburgh).[8] Also, while at Magdalene College, Lewis developed a friendship with the chaplain, Simon Barrington-Ward, later bishop of Coventry.[9]

Lewis's role as an important churchman perhaps culminated in his membership on the Commission to Revise the Psalter for the Prayer Book following Archbishop Geoffrey Fisher's appeal in 1958. Lewis agreed. Together with T. S. Eliot, future archbishop of York Donald Coggan, and three others, Lewis worked on the commission from 1959 until he resigned in August 1963, a few months after the commission completed its revision and four months before his death.[10]

Even after his death, Lewis continues to hold sway among key Anglican theologians, including Bishop N. T. Wright, Archbishop John Semantu, the Rev. Dr. Malcolm Guite, Sir John Polkinghorne,

6. McGrath, *C. S. Lewis*, 241.
7. Farrer, *Faith of Our Own*, 23–43.
8. Lewis, *Collected Letters*, 2:1076–7; Heck, "Chronologically Lewis."
9. Lewis, *Collected Letters*, 2:1471.
10. Heck, "Chronologically Lewis."

Professor Alister McGrath, and Archbishop Rowan Williams, all known for their active engagement with Lewis's work. In these biographical senses, one can count Lewis among Anglicans who think and write fruitfully about theology.

However, neither Lewis's reading and writing nor his active involvement with Anglican theology past and present alone qualify his inclusion among Anglican theologians, for the simple fact that neither his training, his actions, nor his standing serve to qualify him for that title. Indeed, in his first work of apologetics, *The Problem of Pain*, Lewis claims as much in the preface:

> I write, of course, as a layman of the Church of England: but I have tried to assume nothing that is not professed by all baptised and communicating Christians. As this is not a work of erudition I have taken little pains to trace ideas or quotations to their sources when they were not easily recoverable. Any theologian will see easily enough what, and how little, I have read.[11]

Elsewhere he repeats this self-effacing claim concerning his standing in the Anglican Church, calling himself (perhaps with a touch of facetious irony) "a very ordinary layman of the Church of England, not especially 'high,' nor especially 'low,' nor especially anything else."[12] But one must certainly take such a claim with great caution and more than a grain or two of salt, for who could consider "very ordinary" a member of the Anglican Church anyone with the kind of bona fides that Lewis has to offer? Instead of taking such an assertion at face value, it would serve the thoughtful reader to probe more deeply and apply one of Lewis's own standards. For, as he states in *The Four Loves*, the "human mind is generally far more eager to praise and disparage than to describe and define"; perhaps Lewis's work might enjoy more careful consideration once we neither dismiss nor embrace him as a figure but rather seek to define and describe what Lewis did and attempted in his writing.[13]

---

11. Lewis, *Problem of Pain*, xii.
12. Lewis, *Mere Christianity*, viii.
13. Lewis, *Four Loves*, 12.

To do so, to justify the effort to define and describe Lewis as a "theologian," we helpfully turn to Sarah Coakley's considerable first volume of systematics, *God, Sexuality, and the Self*. The remainder of this essay will define Lewis as a theologian in terms Coakley provides and then explore ways in which Lewis's work proleptically embodies several Coakley's hallmarks of *théologie totale*.

In her review of this first of three projected volumes of Coakley's systematic theology, Katherine Sonderegger calls the proposed *théologie totale* of *God, Sexuality, and the Self* "something entirely new," an "altogether dazzling," "disorienting" approach[14] that suggests a "synthetic, organic, integrative," new world of theological expression.[15] True to its title, Coakley proposes that in this *théologie totale* "sociological, literary, art historical and feminist methods stand ready for use" in understanding the nature of God.[16] And one key instance of how Coakley "has renovated the ground of theology" arises from how this *théologie totale* looks outside of theology proper to integrate and unite such disparate elements as Trinitarian theology and sexual desire. To do this, Coakley rejects the assumption that "popular religious movements cannot yield high theological reflection"; in this foundational claim, Coakley makes ample space for what Lewis himself did seventy-five years earlier.[17]

A letter from Lewis to American theologian Carl F. H. Henry in the fall of 1955 crucially supports the argument for Lewis as a theologian, especially considering Coakley's assertion of the transformative power of the imagination and needful iconoclasm. Coakley claims that "if all the faculties and senses (intellect, feeling, will, imagination, aesthetic sensibility) are to be drawn into the realm of the systematic endeavor, then the enormous power of the visual and the imaginative . . . cannot be bypassed or gainsaid."[18]

14. Sonderegger, Review, 94.
15. Sonderegger, Review, 96.
16. Coakley, *God, Sexuality, Self*, 95.
17. Coakley, *God, Sexuality, Self*, 12.
18. Coakley, *God, Sexuality, Self*, 21.

This idea of the theological power of the visual and imaginative would have resonated deeply with Lewis. For in his letter to Henry, Lewis demurs to write (likely) theological and even apologetic articles for the soon-to-premiere evangelical magazine *Christianity Today*, in his profoundly telling reply to Henry:

> I wish your project heartily well but can't write you articles. My thought and talent (such as they are) now flow in different, though I think not less Christian, channels, and I do not think I am at all likely to write more *directly* theological pieces.... If I am now good for anything it is for catching the reader unawares—thro' fiction and symbol. I have done what I could in the way of frontal attacks, but I now feel quite sure those days are over.[19]

Customarily, Lewis understates the importance of his work, a feature of many of his prefaces and introductions. Also customary is his casting of unpleasantness and conflict in terms of his war experiences. But while his tone seems dour to the point of pessimism, his work of the period seems to have given him far more satisfaction than his more direct theological work of the 1940s.

Here Lewis looks back on a decade and a half of writing popular apologetics (*The Problem of Pain*, *Miracles*, *Mere Christianity*, along with several poems, essays, and talks all apologetical in tone) and declares that he can now write only *indirect* theology, and do so by using "fiction and symbol" as a means for "catching the reader unawares" with theological truth. The main works of this period wherein he fulfilled his indirectly theological intentions, *The Chronicles of Narnia* and *Till We Have Faces* (which he called "far and away my best book") seemed to suit his purposes and to satisfy him a great deal, even as they continue to have ongoing spiritual appeal. Arguably, these books have found and continue to enjoy a wider and deeper readership than anything more widely and deeply read than anything he wrote in his more directly theological books of the previous decade.[20]

---

19. Lewis, *Collected Letters*, 3:651.
20. Lewis, *Collected Letters*, 3:1148.

This point is key, and by making it, Lewis in essence anticipates and even undertakes the theological and imaginative task that Coakley describes decades later; she significantly notes that "the contemplative method of *théologie totale* of course already welcomes . . . the arts, as a way into those levels of doctrinal truth, via the imagination and aesthetic artifacts, that more drily intellectual theology often misses," an approach remarkably consonant with Lewis's use of symbol and fiction to communicate theological truth.[21] She goes on quite suggestively to state that

> *théologie totale* thus attends to all the various mediums . . . through which religious truth is expressed aesthetically, whether wordlessly or as "cultural production": it attends to art, to poetry. . . . Through these mediums the realm of the senses can be sharpened, intensified, and then purged and redirected; and through these mediums, also, dimensions of divine truth are evoked which can be found in no other way.[22]

C. S. Lewis would very likely recognize and even hail Coakley's sympathies and methods.

A key connection here comes from Austin Farrer, especially in his Bampton Lectures of 1948 and the second, "The Supernatural and the Weird." In this lecture, Farrer suggests that a "luminous apex" connects the human mind with the supernatural and also explores the way such "religious truth is expressed aesthetically," as Coakley writes, looking to the importance of culture as a means of revelation.[23] Here, we find a helpful ideological conjunction with Coakley, Farrer, and Lewis, who acknowledged reading Farrer's lectures in 1948, the very year he began writing *The Chronicles of Narnia*.[24] One might well imagine that such topics formed part of the twice-weekly meetings of the Inklings, which included Lewis, Farrer, and several others deeply invested in the connection between God, imagination, and human creativity, especially those

---

21. Coakley, *God, Sexuality, Self*, 20–21.
22. Coakley, *God, Sexuality, Self*, 90.
23. Mitchell, *Shared Witness*, 44.
24. Lewis, *Collected Letters*, 3:961.

Inklings mentioned above. Philip Irving Mitchell's book-length study of the "friendship, influence, and Anglican worldview" shared by Lewis and Farrer chronicles many of the ways Farrer's and Lewis's very similar thinking about the theological imagination anticipates and addresses many of Coakley's ideas.[25]

This assertion supports much of Lewis's claim as a theologian. Lewis's ongoing reception as a masterful imaginative writer points to exactly that sort of evocation of divine truth that Coakley suggests. Lewis anticipated this, turning to his native voice of fiction and symbol to do indirect theology in ways that continue to inform the theological imagination at the highest levels. One example will stand in for many: in his 2013 book on the enduring appeal of Narnia, Rowan Williams finds "a strong, coherent spiritual and theological vision" informing Lewis's imaginative work.[26] Williams's claims for and consideration of Lewis's fiction fit seamlessly into Coakley's assertion about artistic, aesthetic, and nontraditional sources of theology and, to a large degree, seem to prove the point. Yes, readers can well look to Lewis as both significantly Anglican and as a significant theologian sui generis.

Establishing this claim in some ways serves as a legitimatizing preface to some of the main work of this essay, which, above all, suggests that by taking Lewis seriously as an Anglican theologian and by continuing to consider and reconsider his works, many of the most central of the "altogether dazzling" suggestions Sarah Coakley makes find vitally significant similarities, if not anticipation, in Lewis's thought. Perhaps the best way to support such a claim comes from exploring the resonances between a number of Coakley's "methodological hallmarks of *théologie totale*," thus demonstrating how a renewed commitment to reading and rediscovering Lewis in his breadth and depth strengthens the understanding of the suggestive profundity of Lewis's work, especially when he is not attempting to write direct theology and apologetics.[27] Lewis's cogent and even proleptic theological thinking should still hold

---

25. See Mitchell, *Shared Witness*, subtitle.
26. Williams, *Lion's World*, 4.
27. Coakley, *God, Sexuality, Self*, 88–92.

a firm place in the kinds of conversations and interrogations that Coakley initiates.

In her work, Coakley begins by "privileging contemplation," asserting that "radical attention to the Real," especially in contemplation, offers a uniquely helpful approach to the Trinity.[28] And she finds ready agreement from Lewis. She asserts that "silence of contemplation is the incubator for the strength and courage" to resist the horrors of the world, and as such, that silence offers to those who will pause and pray a way to get near to the source "of infinite tenderness and joy; and we learn to endure the ongoing noetic slippage that ever reminds us of that fact, and . . . that dazzles us with its unspeakable presence"; this assertion echoes much of what Lewis wrote about his deeply-developed prayer life.[29]

Lewis's deep commitment to his prayer life formed him at a fundamental level. While he would not consider himself an ascetic, nevertheless, he seems to understand quite well, both experientially and intellectually, the later implications and ideas in this first hallmark of Coakley's. Near the end of his life, he says this about silent prayer: "I still think the prayer without words is the best," although to "pray successfully without words one needs to be at the top of one's form,'" a rare enough occasion for him. But when "the golden moments come, when God enables one really to pray without words, who but a fool would reject the gift?"[30] He found "prayers without words the best" when he could manage it; he made it one of his four rules about his prayers to "pray without words when I am able."[31] Lewis certainly valued contemplative, wordless prayer as its highest form.

Indeed, the dazzling "unspeakability" Coakley describes makes a signal appearance in Lewis's fiction, especially in his last novel, *Till We Have Faces*. In this book, which in many ways anticipates most of Coakley's concerns, the main character, Orual, has spent all of her life railing against the false images of gods she

---

28. Coakley, *God, Sexuality, Self*, 88.
29. Coakley, *God, Sexuality, Self*, 326.
30. Lewis, *Letters to Malcolm*, 11.
31. Lewis, *Letters to Malcolm*, 237, 500.

had set up. But the gods of the novel (tellingly Eros and Aphrodite) eventually dismantle all her complaints about their cruelty, and in the very last pages, it dawns on Orual that these false images have betrayed her, that she is guilty of making false idols out of real gods. When she finally becomes aware of the love of even these pagan gods in a pre-incarnational culture, it overwhelms her. She surrenders then her book-length complaint against them and can add only that joy silenced her.[32] The last words Orual writes find her caught up in divine love she finally both realizes and returns, but even these words end up obscured by her head, which covers them. Effectively, she demonstrates an almost literal example of the kind of "noetic slippage" Coakley suggests; she bows her head to the love that has pursued her, head, heart, and soul, throughout the novel. Lewis thus ends what he called "far and away my best book" with words of love for the god of love, words essentially of silent adoration, an experience even more recognizable because of Coakley's suggestions.[33]

Orual, throughout the novel, has been plagued by her own desires, apparently frustrated by the gods, specifically the tribal equivalents of Eros and Aphrodite. These frustrations lead to her book-length complaint; only a careful reading, especially of book 2, reveals that her desires have actually been tools that the gods consistently offered to Orual to help her see divine love operative in her own life, a concept she shields herself against to the point of spiritual blindness. Much hinges on her refusal to see or acknowledge any connection between her own desires, the love and wooing of the gods, and a troubling question of vision, particularly near the middle of the book. She unaccountably hears the divine voice asking why her heart should not dance, but this invitation to joy fills her with a desire she quickly and cynically quashes.[34]

Coakley's second hallmark, "theology *in via*," refers to "attentive openness of the whole self and the 'interruption' of the Spirit," which "involves an ongoing journey of purgative transformation

---

32. Lewis, *Till We Have Faces*, 306.
33. Lewis, *Collected Letters*, 3:1181; *Till We Have Faces*, 308.
34. Lewis, *Till We Have Faces*, 96.

and change."[35] And such an ongoing conversion process leading to such self-integration seems to describe Lewis's post-conversion life well. Many biographers have noted as much, taking to heart what Walter Hooper, Lewis's personal secretary, has claimed about Lewis: "Lewis struck me as the most thoroughly converted man I ever met. Christianity was never for him a separate department of life.... His whole vision of life was such that the natural and the supernatural seemed inseparably combined."[36] This combination seems to define just the sort of ongoing journey that Coakley suggests. Alister McGrath agrees, pointing to Lewis as one who exemplified that "when rightly understood, the Christian faith could integrate reason, longing, and imagination," again suggesting the kind of progressive cohesion that Coakley's *théologie totale* involves.[37]

When discussing her third hallmark, "the counterpoint of philosophy, science, and *théologie totale*," Coakley asserts that "theology's 'reason'... is both purified and *expanded* by the dark purgation of contemplation," allowing it to "remain in contrapuntal discussion with secular philosophy and science," an idea that Lewis both embodied and embraced.[38] Lewis's prayer life begins as soon as he converts to theism and continues by all accounts for the rest of his life (any small sampling of his voluminous letters attests to this). Already a brilliant academic and a holder of three Firsts from Oxford, perhaps the best evidence of this hallmark comes from Lewis's involvement as president in the 1940s of the Oxford Socratic Club, a group devoted to open debate between educated and thoughtful voices of atheism and Christianity. Detailing Lewis's apologetic role in those meetings, Austin Farrer praises Lewis at some length for offering "a positive exhibition of the force of Christian ideas, morally, imaginatively, and rationally"; often Lewis did so against non-Christian proponents of just the kind

---

35. Coakley, *God, Sexuality, Self*, 88.
36. Lewis, *God in the Dock*, 12.
37. McGrath, *C. S. Lewis*, 88.
38. Coakley, *God, Sexuality, Self*, 89; emphasis in original.

of "secular philosophy and science" Coakley discusses.³⁹ Lewis's prayer-soaked rationalism made him, at his height, one of the most essential apologists of the twentieth century.

Should we regard Coakley's work as apologetic? Not directly so, but perhaps as another species of the kind of indirectly apologetic work Lewis intended in his fiction. We can certainly see in both authors a deepening urge to enter theologically into scientific and philosophical conversations with a theological approach, repertoire, and vocabulary that, if credible, makes a very viable case for the importance of the divine or at least a thoughtful divine lens, among the going concerns and topics of the intellectual climate. And in this, we might well look not only to Queen Esther but also to her biblical book as a species (broadly) of what Lewis and Coakley attempt to do. We find that we do not need to hear directly the name of God to see God's hand at work through a praying person, even in the palaces of power in Queen Esther's day. So too, both Lewis and Coakley assert that theological language can escape its disciplinary confines, especially if a person of faith seeks to use it to offer a de facto defense of vibrant, viable, relevant Christianity.

Regarding her fourth hallmark, "orthodoxy as a goal," Coakley seeks a "horizon of true orthodoxy" at which "theology, 'spirituality,' and ethics are fully united" as a result of "personal transformation in response to divine truth."⁴⁰ With such a description, one might almost suspect that Coakley has in mind the example of Lewis, especially as the author of *Mere Christianity*, which in one volume offers at least a starting point towards those very goals; that book's ongoing appeal indeed suggests Lewis's continuing success at capturing this kind of united orthodoxy. Certainly, McGrath finds in that book "what Lewis believed the Church of England to represent at its best . . . the historic orthodox Christian faith as it found expression in England," an apt description of Lewis's intentions.⁴¹

---

39. Farrer, "Christian Apologist," 26; Coakley, *God, Sexuality, Self*, 89.
40. Coakley, *God, Sexuality, Self*, 88–89.
41. McGrath, *C. S. Lewis*, 220; Lewis, *Mere Christianity*, vii.

Coakley's fifth hallmark, "*théologie totale* as socially located but not socially reduced," offers readers a kind of two-pronged opportunity to address common, though fairly misinformed, complaints about Lewis. In stating that her approach "applies the hermeneutics of suspicion" as well as, ultimately, "the hermeneutics of charity and hope," she sounds themes familiar to readers who would take Lewis's work seriously.[42] Lewis's educational upbringing inculcated in him just such an attitude of suspicion; his education was guided by teachers and editors who "took it for granted from the outset that [pagan] religious ideas were sheer illusion." From them, Lewis drew the impression "that religion in general, though utterly false, was a natural growth, a kind of endemic nonsense into which humanity tended to blunder," using the key of a kind of dismissive suspicion that unlocked the door out of religion, much to the relief of the skeptical teenaged Lewis.[43] However, this training, along with the rigorous dialectic of his education in his teens and twenties, ultimately led him through such suspicions and years of rational struggles, leading to his conversion first to theism, then to Christianity, and, ultimately, to hope and charity. Lewis, too, "discerningly adjudicated" his social and philosophical world in coming to believe in God and ardently practice Christianity.[44]

Coakley's sixth hallmark, that *théologie totale* leads to "the expansion of the classic systematic loci," finds a ready participant in Lewis, especially as an author of fiction.[45] Coakley argues for a systematic theology that changes traditional approaches, which she describes as "unsystematic systematics," characterized by particular and complex attention to questions of gender, race, and class as it seeks to improve human beings.[46] And Lewis, too, attends to such questions at least seminally, despite those myopic and shallow readings of some critics who too often reflexively charge him

---

42. Coakley, *God, Sexuality, Self*, 90.
43. Lewis, *Surprised by Joy*, 75.
44. Coakley, *God, Sexuality, Self*, 90.
45. Coakley, *God, Sexuality, Self*, 90.
46. Coakley, *God, Sexuality, Self*, 60.

with misogyny and racism. These charges ultimately prove far too facile and, in the main, unsubstantial when examined more closely. Lewis, too, was deeply interested in difference and shows an arc of change and growth throughout his writings and thinking on just such questions. In Narnia, for instance, one sees an increase of female characters, and women and girls (one would do well to remember that most of the females Lewis portrays are preadolescent) often occupy positions of more significant power and vision than their male counterparts. In several of the chronicles, Lucy, for example, offers the kind of rare insight and perspicacity that Lewis seemed to hope to inspire in all readers. In Aravis (in *The Horse and His Boy*), we find an apparently Middle Eastern girl gifted in storytelling and often the holder of the wisest perspectives. Emeth (in *The Last Battle*), too, hails from the obviously Middle Eastern land of Calormen, replete with people of dark skin, scimitars, and pointed shoes. But the young warrior's name in Hebrew means "truth," and he offers one of the best examples of courage and noble character. Those seeking out benighted attitudes about gender, race, and class will find them in Lewis mostly by projecting their own presuppositional attitudes, turning a blind eye towards what he actually was doing, and not attending nearly critically enough to the actual text and Lewis's far-reaching project.

Issues of sexuality in particular have garnered some important consideration, much of which is profitably explored in such volumes as *Women and C. S. Lewis* and *A Sword Between the Sexes? C. S. Lewis and the Gender Debates*, and less helpfully so in *Women Among the Inklings: Gender, C. S. Lewis, J. R. R. Tolkien, and Charles Williams*.[47] In the end, careful attention to Lewis, both personally and in his writings, reveals him as a man eager for and open to growth in his understanding. Throughout his lifetime and throughout his corpus, Lewis demonstrates an appreciation of difference in ways that merit more consideration that many have afforded him.

---

47. Curtis and Key, *Women and C. S. Lewis*; Van Leeuwen, *Sword Between the Sexes*; Fredrick and McBride, *Women Among the Inklings*.

"Joy Silenced Me"

As briefly noted, Narnia offers a particular locus for unsystematic systematics. Much has rightly been made about the Christological implications of Aslan, of which Michael Ward's recent book *Planet Narnia* is perhaps the best. Few could argue that Lewis was making profoundly theological statements about the Son of God in the leonine person of Aslan. However, mentions of the other two persons of the Trinity remain nearly nonexistent in the seven books. True to his claim that, in the chronicles, he in no way "hammered out 'allegories'" for a list of Christian truths, the depth of the Christological considerations begs questions about nearly nonexistent pneumatology and Trinitarian elements in Narnia.[48] His failures in some areas of systematics conjoined with his successes in others seem just those sort of "fresh ways" Coakley envisions in her *théologie totale*.[49]

Admittedly, one might wish Lewis spoke and wrote more often and more directly about the Holy Trinity, as Coakley certainly does. The closest Lewis gets appears in *Mere Christianity*:

> This third Person [of the Trinity] is called, in technical language, the Holy Ghost or the "spirit" of God. Do not be worried or surprised if you find it (or Him) rather vaguer or more shadowy in your mind than the other two. I think there is a reason why that must be so. In the Christian life you are not usually looking at Him. He is always acting through you. If you think of the Father as something "out there," in front of you, and of the Son as someone standing at your side, helping you to pray, trying to turn you into another son, then you have to think of the third Person as something inside you, or behind you.[50]

This passage comes from the chapter "Good Infection," which follows "The Three-Personal God," perhaps Lewis's best attempt to explain the doctrine popularly, initially for an eleven-minute BBC broadcast. And while Lewis acknowledges his very initial efforts,

---

48. Lewis, "Sometimes Fairy Stories," 46.
49. Coakley, *God, Sexuality, Self*, 90.
50. Lewis, *Mere Christianity*, 175–76.

subtitling book 4 of *Mere Christianity* "First Steps in the Doctrine of the Trinity," Coakley certainly begins much farther down this road than where Lewis leaves off. But perhaps it reflects on the argument for Lewis as theologian that we would gladly hear him say much more.

The penultimate hallmark, the "overcoming of false divides," finds a deep resonance in Lewis's own theology. In addition to his notion (discussed above) of seeking to define and describe rather than praise or dispraise, Lewis also helps readers to overcome false divides in *Mere Christianity*. He remarks that "so many people ... like thinking in terms of good and bad, not of good, better, and best, or bad, worse and worst"; in doing so, Lewis appears very much to share cause with Coakley as she presses readers away from false dyads and binaries and towards true Trinitarian thinking.[51]

Furthering the above remarks concerning Lewis's attitudes towards women, one finds if one reads carefully enough attitudes, one might be shocked by how they help tear down divides of gender. In *That Hideous Strength*, the last of Lewis's interplanetary romances, the narrator asserts that Mercury and Mars represent masculine genders. In contrast, Venus represents the feminine, much as one might expect. But then, in a sadly overlooked and highly suggestive comment, Lewis's narrator goes on to suggest that other planets represent others of the "*seven Genders*."[52] In a letter to Dorothy L. Sayers, he claimed not to "like either the ultra-feminine or the ultra-masculine myself. I prefer people."[53] While much more could (and perhaps should) be said about how these statements bear on Lewis's complex and unfolding views on gender throughout his life, these two statements are enough to underscore his sympathy with Coakley's project of dismantling false binaries through careful Trinitarian thinking.

Lewis and Coakley's closest point of contact comes in her ninth and last hallmark, "desire as the constellating theological category of *théologie totale*"; at the end, we arrive at perhaps the

---

51. Lewis, *Mere Christianity*, 108.
52. Lewis, *That Hideous Strength*, 322; emphasis added.
53. Lewis, *Collected Letters*, 3:639.

heart of Coakley's thesis: the importance of sexual desire as integral to an understanding of the Trinity. She began her book with the claim that

> no cogent answer to the contemporary Christian question of the Trinitarian God can be given without charting the necessary and intrinsic entanglement of human sexuality and spirituality in such a quest: the questions of right contemplation of God, right speech about God, and right ordering of desire all hang together.

This last hallmark proves maybe the most important to the argument for Lewis as an Anglican theologian worth careful rediscovery, consideration, (re-)reading, and perhaps even deliberate rehabilitation within current theological conversations.[54] The concept of desire, especially as related to the divine, occupies an extremely central role in Lewis's theological approach. Lewis and Coakley essentially begin at the same place, draw the same conclusions, and reach the same ends, though divided by their different disciplines, and more than half a century.

What Coakley discusses as "desire," Lewis calls "Joy" (*Sehnsucht*), and it remains a central theme in understanding his approach to theology. In defining what he calls Joy and Coakley calls desire, Lewis describes the experience as "one of intense longing," a "sweet Desire [which] cuts across our ordinary distinctions between wanting and having," which serves to point ultimately to God.[55] And while the theme echoes through most of Lewis's work, he speaks most powerfully about it in his various attempts at autobiography. These attempts, along with his grappling with the relation of desire or Joy and its relationship to God, span Lewis's life and publishing career. It is perhaps no overstatement to claim that Lewis's pursuit of Joy and its fulfillment occupied the central place in his life.

But in Lewis's approach to this desire (however one terms it), we find a clue that aligns him closely, not only with Coakley but

---

54. Coakley, *God, Sexuality, Self*, 92.
55. Lewis, *Pilgrim's Regress*, 209–10.

with what we may consider in some senses the very heart of Christian theology, namely, the love of God. For Lewis, desire, especially sexual desire, plays a significant role in his theology of Joy. Perhaps one finds this in his recently published first spiritual biography, which recounts his conversion to theism (and not yet, by the end, to Christianity). "Early Prose Joy," even more than his other attempts at spiritual autobiography, makes plain the role of desire in Lewis's grappling with God.

This idea reaches some maturity in the last chapter (titled intriguingly "The Beginning") of Lewis's best-known spiritual autobiography, *Surprised by Joy*, in which Lewis determines that desire finds its telos in the God of love. As he concludes his book and sums up his central ideas, Lewis speaks of the futility of desire as an end in itself, instead querying:

> But what, in conclusion, of Joy? for that, after all, is what the story has mainly been about. To tell you the truth, the subject has lost nearly all interest for me since I became a Christian. . . . I believe . . . that the old stab, the old bittersweet, has come to me as often and as sharply since my conversion as at any time of my life whatever. But I now know that the experience . . . had never had the kind of importance I once gave it. It was valuable only as a pointer to something other and outer.[56]

What is this "other and outer" to which desire points? The key clue comes in the audio recordings that served as the first draft of *The Four Loves*, where we find Lewis's crucial definition of love as that move "in which we *go out of ourself towards others*."[57] Therefore, desire, or Joy, points to the other, the outer. In a word, this desire with which Lewis grappled all his life finally resolved itself into love, and especially the love of God. And in this crucial theological move, Lewis's literary theology lines up very neatly indeed with Sarah Coakley's *théologie totale*, especially regarding her concern with the relation of subject and object in desire; certainly, we have

---

56. Lewis, *Surprised by Joy*, 291.
57. Lewis, *Four Loves*, track 1, "Storge," 4:47.

enough to place Lewis in serious theological conversation with Coakley, and, logically, many other theologians.

Much more could be said, for Coakley's ideas on almost every page find resonance and solid examples in Lewis's work. No mention has been made about a myriad of other connections: Lewis's apophatic approach; his commitment to *ekstasis* as a theologically reliable epistemological element; his deliberate connection between spiritual principle and personal practice; the role and interrelations of Venus, Eros, and Agape; his ideas of vision; his claims, published and unpublished, about the iconoclastic nature of reality. But ultimately, Orual, in his last novel, has the last, lost word. With her, Lewis could accurately claim that, in his pursuit of that desire that had brought him to the point where all his questions died away before the face of the God of Love, Joy silenced him. And following much silent contemplation of the love of God that constitutes the nature of the Holy Trinity, Coakley and Lewis could have long and fruitful discussions.

And so, even beyond Lewis's background in and involvement with Anglicans of previous centuries and his, Lewis still holds his place today in many of the most significant and creative theological conversations, not the least of which is Sarah Coakley's redoubtable and promising thinking, with which Lewis held so very much in common.

Bibliography

Coakley, Sarah. *God, Sexuality, and the Self: An Essay "On the Trinity."* 5th ed. Cambridge: Cambridge University Press, 2015.

Curtis, Carolyn, and Mary Pomroy Key. *Women and C. S. Lewis: What His Life and Literature Reveal for Today's Culture.* Oxford, UK: Lion, 2015.

Farrer, Austin. "The Christian Apologist." In *Light on C. S. Lewis*, edited by Jocelyn Gibb, 23–43. New York: Harcourt, Brace & World, 1965.

———. *A Faith of Our Own.* Cleveland: World, 1960.

Fredrick, Candace, and Sam McBride. *Women Among the Inklings: Gender, C. S. Lewis, J. R. R. Tolkien, and Charles Williams.* Contributions in Women's Studies. Westport, CT: Greenwood, 2001.

Green, Roger Lancelyn, and Walter Hooper. *C. S. Lewis: A Biography.* Rev. ed. San Diego: Harvest, 1994.

Heck, Joel. "Chronologically Lewis." Joel Heck, Apr. 15, 2025. https://joelheck.com/chronologically-lewis/.

Lewis, C. S. *Collected Letters.* Edited by Walter Hooper. 3 vols. San Francisco: Harper San Francisco, 2005-7.

———. "'Early Prose Joy': C. S. Lewis's Early Draft of an Autobiographical Manuscript." *VII: Journal of the Marion E. Wade Center* 30 (2013) 13–50. https://www.jstor.org/stable/48599471.

———. *English Literature in the Sixteenth Century, Excluding Drama.* Oxford History of English Literature. Oxford: Clarendon, 1954.

———. *The Four Loves.* Recorded Aug. 19, 1958. Grand Haven, MI: Brilliance Audio, 2005. Compact disc.

———. *The Four Loves.* New York: Harcourt, 1960.

———. *God in the Dock: Essays on Theology and Ethics.* Edited by Walter Hooper. Grand Rapids: Eerdmans, 1987.

———. *The Horse and His Boy.* New York: HarperCollins, 2005.

———. *The Last Battle.* New York: HarperCollins, 1956.

———. *Letters to Malcolm: Chiefly on Prayer.* New York: Harcourt, 1964.

———. *Mere Christianity.* New York: HarperOne, 1952.

———. *The Pilgrim's Regress.* Edited by David C. Downing. Wade Annotated ed. Grand Rapids: Eerdmans, 2014.

———. *The Problem of Pain.* New York: HarperOne, 1940.

———. "Sometimes Fairy Stories May Say Best What's to Be Said." In *"On Stories" and Other Essays on Literature*, edited by Walter Hooper, 45–48. New York: Harcourt Brace Jovanovich, 1982.

———. *Surprised by Joy: The Shape of My Early Life.* San Francisco: HarperOne, 2017.

———. *That Hideous Strength: A Modern Fairy-Tale for Grown-Ups.* Vol. 3 of *The Cosmic Trilogy.* New York: Scribner, 2003.

McGrath, Alister. *C. S. Lewis: A Life; Eccentric Genius, Reluctant Prophet.* Carol Stream, IL: Tyndale, 2013.

———. "Lewis's Appeal to the Imagination." *Church Times*, Nov. 15, 2013. http://www.churchtimes.co.uk/articles/2013/15-november/features/features/lewis-s-appeal-to-the-imagination.

Mitchell, Philip Irving. *The Shared Witness of C. S. Lewis and Austin Farrer: Friendship, Influence, and an Anglican Worldview*. Kent, OH: Kent State University Press, 2021.

Smith, Sandy. "Surprised by Belfast: Significant Sites in the Life of C. S. Lewis—Part 3." C. S. Lewis Institute, Sept. 5, 2016. http://www.cslewisinstitute.org/Surprised_by_Belfast_Significant_Sites_in_the_Life_of_CS_Lewis_Part_III_St_Marks_Church_Holywood_Road_FullArticle.

Sonderegger, Katherine. Review of *God, Sexuality, and the Self*, by Sarah Coakley. *International Journal of Systematic Theology* 18 (2016) 94–98. https://doi.org/10.1111/ijst.12132.

Van Leeuwen, Mary Stewart. *A Sword Between the Sexes? C. S. Lewis and the Gender Debates*. Grand Rapids: Brazos, 2010.

Ward, Michael. *Planet Narnia: The Seven Heavens in the Imagination of C. S. Lewis*. Oxford: Oxford University Press, 2008.

Williams, Rowan. *The Lion's World: A Journey into the Heart of Narnia*. Oxford: Oxford University Press, 2012.

4

"But Only Say the Word, And I Shall Be Healed"

Conversion in the Writings of C. S. Lewis

Tricia Lyons

I come to the question of conversion to faith through the writings of C. S. Lewis not from mere academic curiosity. This essay attempts to explore what, for Lewis, religious conversion to faith in God is and how it happens. It also explores why it might be that so many people have credited works by C. S. Lewis for their own conversions to Christianity and/or to a deeper experience of it. I have spent over thirty years trying to understand in philosophical and theological frameworks how it was that hearing a person read to me a portion of *The Chronicles of Narnia* in the fall of 1991 brought about one of the most profound conversions in my life to a personal relationship with Jesus Christ.

I was a freshman at Harvard College and in the fall of that first year, my father died an early death after a years-long decline from poor health and alcoholism. I left college for a few days to attend his funeral and returned by train to Cambridge the very night of that funeral. I wanted so desperately to move on but didn't know how. I came back that night to a dorm suite of four other roommates who were polite but clearly awkward that their new friend had just buried her father that day. I went into my private bedroom to be alone. The resident advisor came to my door and asked to sit with me. She had clearly been alerted to my return. I didn't know her name, though I remembered she was a graduate student in divinity. She was utterly kind and reassuring that the college would do anything to help me in this time of mourning. I had few words. Before leaving, she asked if she could read me a story. I looked at her for the first time. I found this an odd request. I said something wry like "You mean a bedtime story?" Her powerful peacefulness was unphased by my sarcasm. She asked again. I said, "Sure." With no introduction, she proceeded to read from *The Voyage of the Dawn Treader*. She read me the story of Eustace, and how he became a dragon and how he became a boy again. She read for about ten minutes (or was it hours?) skipping a page here and there to get the core of the story out of two chapters in the book. The story grabbed my heart so tightly that my breath was racing. I had never heard this story. And yet, I felt it was my life told in another time.

Although I was only eighteen years old, my father's death was the second in my immediate family, my having lost my only sister to a car accident a decade before. Her death exacerbated the financial instability, the grief of generational poverty, and the alcoholism that clouded our home. Like Eustace, I had put on scales to protect myself from the cruelty and pain of my world. I too had tried to pull off those scales for years. I too was choking on my thirst and my limbs also ached with the burden of my desperation. But then I heard the RA change the tone of her voice as she read of Aslan's appearance, his removal of the scales that trapped the sad dragon, and his transformation of Eustace back into a boy. She smiled and left my room without adding a single word to the reading. Never in my short life had I—all of a sudden— wanted something so badly. I slept only a few hours and then walked at sunrise to the bank of the Charles River. I sat on a bench by the water on that November Sunday (the Feast of All Saints) not far from the entrance to what

I now know is the monastery of the Society of St. John the Evangelist. Something had already happened to me. To hear of an un-dragoning had removed my own scales. To hear of Aslan's redemption was to have experienced it. I was a new person. I could feel it. And there were also a thousand heavy loads and torments that I could no longer feel at all. That was not the beginning of my faith, but it was the end of my life as merely a "religious person" or member of a church. It was the end of thinking about God without also feeling redemption moving and transforming my body and imagination into the Triune Life. I always believed I would be resurrected. But it never occurred to me—until it happened to me—that it could start while I was still alive.

Despite my own frustrations and criticisms of Lewis that have grown as I have in intersectional living and learning, I live with and by the fact that God used Lewis's writings to convert my heart from stone to flesh. And so, I continue, out of joyful gratitude and authentic witness, to declare the power of reading Lewis in this and any age.

Many questions are raised by the word "conversion," such as what specifically are the "needs" that people are responding to, how do we become aware of them, and what do they mean? And what, if anything, *does* the human need? There is also a tension that exists in theories of conversion that identify both human and divine agency. This tension raises questions such as, what is the impact of one agent on the other? What are the dynamics of this dialectic, and what are the limits of the human and divine will to affect one another? If conversion is a choice, whose choice, is it? A clear discussion of the supernatural and its relation to the human will in the act and process of conversion is necessary to clarify any view of conversion that includes, implicitly or explicitly, a notion of divine intervention.

C. S. Lewis acknowledges and addresses the aforementioned tension between the role of the human will and the role of a divine will in conversion. According to Lewis, the divine agent demonstrates, through a variety of intrusions into the natural world, the need and the possibility of conversion, but ultimately the conversion process is determined by a willingness in the human to change and surrender his or her autonomy. The dialectic begins with an invitation to a relationship posed by the divine; in conversion the invitation is accepted by the individual.

Lewis grounds his exploration of the relationship between man and supernatural forces in a clear notion of the human being. He argues that in addition to the natural laws that govern the physical world (such as gravity or mathematical laws) all people have an innate awareness of an objective, moral law. Lewis calls this law the Law of Human Nature. This law is an objective standard which, he argues, can be found in one form or another in all cultures and in all religions.

> It is the doctrine of objective value, the belief that certain attitudes are really true, and others really false, to the kind of thing the universe is and the kind of things we are. Those who know [the law] can hold that to call children delightful or old men venerable is not simply to record a psychological fact about our own parental or filial emotions at the moment, but to recognize a quality which *demands* a certain response from us whether we make it or not. . . . And because our approvals and disapprovals are thus recognitions of objective value or responses to an objective order, therefore emotional states can be in harmony with reason (when we feel liking for what ought to be approved) or out of harmony with reason (when we perceive that liking is due but cannot feel it).[1]

Lewis argues that "reason" is a human faculty that recognizes the reality of the law and informs the individual of it. When one becomes aware of the law, the result is an awareness of the freedom of the will to accept or reject the law—for unlike gravity or mathematical laws, this law can be transgressed by an act of the will. The reality of the Law of Human Nature is experienced when humans become aware of their freedom to either adopt or reject the moral law. But although one experiences freedom when exercising the

---

1. Lewis, *Abolition of Man*, 7.

will, experience also demonstrates that humans are not free to feel whatever they want about their choices. Transgression of the law challenges one's reason and impresses the individual with the sense that they could have acted otherwise. Lewis argues,

> [H]uman beings, all over the earth, have this curious idea that they ought to behave in a certain way, and cannot really get rid of it . . . [and] that they do not in fact behave in that way. They know the Law of Human Nature; they break it. These two facts are the foundation of all clear thinking about ourselves and the universe we live in.[2]

Individuals are free to make choices, but not free to set the boundaries within which they will feel comfortable with these choices. Humans will experience a tension if their actions are not in harmony with the Law of Human Nature. Lewis argues that when the Law of Human Nature is transgressed, the human experiences a tension with his reason for having done so. As a result of the Law of Human Nature, man realizes that his freedom exists within a fixed field of moral absolutes. We are free to transgress, but not to create objective, moral law. It is this realization—that humans are free to act and not to set the standards for moral action—that is essential to the onset of the conversion process. Conversion is a process that begins with the acknowledgment that there are objective absolutes with which man can either harmonize his life and choices, or remain in discord. Lewis describes this realization, saying, "when I open that particular man called Myself, I find that I do not exist on my own, that I am under a law; that somebody or something wants me to behave in a certain way."[3]

It is this tension between an awareness of freedom and the experienced reality of an objective standard, that creates in man a need for further consideration of the nature of that standard and its author. Lewis states, "we have to assume [objective morality] is more like a mind than it is like anything else we know—because after all the only other thing we know is matter and you can hardly

---

2. Lewis, *Mere Christianity*, 7.
3. Lewis, *Mere Christianity*, 20.

imagine a bit of matter giving instructions."[4] And so through tension caused by violation of the moral law, man becomes aware of a set of moral standards that points to a kind of supernatural "mind" or personality. Our reason is endowed with a sense of duty to legislate and bring forth the moral law as the standard for the human will. If this is not done, the individual feels a sense of discord or separation with the "mind" behind the moral law. Lewis, in his discussion of the Law of Human Nature, explains how this possibility is presented to the individual. Objective morality communicates to man that he is able only to acknowledge the standard and not to alter it. Consequent feelings of isolation and guilt when the moral law is transgressed prove to man that he stands within the edifice of objective morality as the guest and not the architect. Lewis presents this realization as a first step toward conversion. It is, as it were, humanity's first encounter with the mind behind objective reality.

One metaphor Lewis employs to describe this longing caused by human desire to reconcile with the source of law is the image of a "far-off country," implying that experience of the supernatural imprints in humanity a vision that its rightful citizenship is in a reality beyond the purely natural world. Lewis states,

> In speaking of this desire for our own far-off country, which we find in ourselves even now, I feel a certain shyness. I am almost committing an indecency. I am trying to rip open the inconsolable secret in each one of you—the secret which hurts so much that you take your revenge on it by calling it names like Nostalgia and Romanticism and Adolescence.... We cannot tell it because it is a desire for something that has never actually appeared in our experience. We cannot hide it because our experience is constantly suggesting it.... Our commonest expedient is to call it beauty and behave as if we have settled the matter.... The books or the music in which we thought the beauty was located will betray us if

---

4. Lewis, *Mere Christianity*, 20.

we trust to them; it was not *in* them, it only came *through* them, and what came through them was longing.[5]

Man's constant interaction with these intrusions of the infinite and the supernatural results in a longing to reach that far-off country, to experience harmony with, and citizenship within, the a supernatural reality. According to Lewis,

> These things—the beauty, the memory of our own past— are good images of what we really desire; but if they are mistaken for the thing itself, they turn into dumb idols, breaking the hearts of their worshippers. For they are not the thing in itself; they are only the scent of a flower we have not found, the echo of a tune we have not heard, news from a country we have never yet visited.[6]

This universal sense of longings is, for Lewis, the evidence for something beyond nature. The longing is accompanied by images that introduce our thoughts to possible explanations of it. These images, such as a "far-off country," are constructs that work in response to reason which postulates their reality. In this way, the imagination operates to paint the picture that reason posits. Intrusions of the supernatural that produce images that do not correspond to direct experiences occur at moments of guilt, loneliness, love, joy, frustration, and other emotions. Lewis argues that this longing is either a malfunction of the human mind or it is a message. In other words, either the imagination fools us with images or else these images are an attempt to construct a picture of an unseen reality. Longings are the imprint of an objective reality that, alone, can fulfill them. Images are a direct result of longing, an attempt to envision a fulfillment of the reality which makes the imprint. Lewis states,

> "Creatures are not born with desires unless satisfaction for those desires exists. A baby feels hunger: well, there is such a thing as food. A duckling wants to swim: well, there is such a thing as water. Men feel sexual desire: well,

5. Lewis, *Weight of Glory*, 30.
6. Lewis, *Weight of Glory*, 31.

there is such a thing as sex. If I find in myself a desire which no experience in this world can satisfy, the most probable explanation is that I was made for another world . . . earthly pleasures were never meant to satisfy [this longing] but only to arouse it, to suggest the real thing.[7]

Lewis adds that one must not "mistake [longing] for the something else of which they are only a kind of copy, or echo, or mirage." The human imagination is innately occupied with thoughts of the infinite and of the transcendent; thoughts and images with no direct corresponding object in this world. Therefore, consciousness itself becomes a struggle to identify what is real about experiences with the supernatural.

Lewis, in an essay entitled "Meditation in a Toolshed," presents a bifocal approach for understanding phenomena. In the essay, Lewis discusses two different ways of looking at a beam of light shining through a hole in the ceiling of a toolshed. One perspective looks directly at a section of the beam as it appears in the shed, considering the particles which make up the light. Lewis calls this approach looking "at" the light. The second perspective is to look "along" the light, which includes seeing all objects in the shed as effected by the light. Lewis states that taking the second perspective resulted in an entirely different experience of the beam. "Instead I saw, framed in the irregular cranny in the top of the door, green leaves moving on the branches of a tree outside and beyond that, 90 odd million miles away, the sun."[8] Looking "at" something reveals what the thing is; looking "along" seeks to determine what the thing means, what its origins are, and what is its boundaries or boundlessness.

Looking *at*, therefore, results in existential judgments; looking *along* reveals the spiritual judgments of meaning and origin. Looking *along* a phenomenon implies a certain involvement or immersion in the experience. Looking *along* the beam of light requires that an individual step into the light and see the external

---

7. Lewis, *Mere Christianity*, 106.
8. Lewis, "Meditation in a Toolshed," 230.

world from within the beam. According to Lewis, "You get one experience of a thing when you look along it and another when you look at it. Which is the 'true' or 'valid' experience? Which tells you most about the thing?"[9] Lewis does not say that one judgment is perpetually superior to the other, but defends the view that looks along in saying that one cannot "[taken] for granted that the external account of a thing somehow refutes or 'debunks' the account given from inside." Lewis argues that invaluable insight can be gained by seeing a phenomenon from within the experience of it. Without some notion of the "inside" view of an experience, one's thoughts are only speculation. They are not based on any impression one has received from direct experience.

Lewis's view of looking *along* and looking *at* offer a possible resolution to the issue of the role of a free will in the conversion process. It is not difficult to reconcile the freedom of the individual will and the presence of an objective moral law. Man is free to act either in accordance with or in transgression of the standard. But surely conversion is not simply a result of becoming aware of an objective morality. Clearly, there is more that the individual is responding to, more of an experience with the supernatural that convinces him of the reality of the divine and of a possible relationship with it. To look at the Law of Human Nature shows an individual what is and what is not right; looking along the Law of Human Nature leads the individual to consider its origins and its meaning.

At the time of his conversion, Lewis was influenced by the work of philosopher S. Alexander. Much of Lewis's notion of this bifocal approach to phenomena is derived from Alexander's philosophy found in *Space, Time, and Deity*.[10] Lewis cites Alexander as having dramatically influenced his own thought. Alexander defines two technical terms in his notion of the human will: contemplating and enjoying. Lewis summarizes Alexander's philosophy: "When you see a table you 'enjoy' the act of seeing and 'contemplate' the table." *Enjoying* is taking part in the object; *contemplating*

---

9. Lewis, "Meditation in a Toolshed," 231.
10. Alexander, *Space, Time, and Deity*, 11–12.

"But Only Say the Word, and I Shall Be Healed"

is the thought of the process of seeing or experiencing the object. These two processes are exclusive of one another; it is not possible to enjoy and contemplate an experience or object at the same moment. "You cannot hope," states Lewis, "and also think about hoping at the same moment; for in hope we look to hope's object and we interrupt this by (so to speak) turning round to look at the hope itself . . . the two activities . . . are distinct and incompatible." This distinction was crucial for Lewis in the process of his own religious conversion. Contemplating these two modes of analysis led him to discover that his longing came from an object that he had not, until that point, acknowledged. His interaction with his longing had "been a futile attempt to contemplate the enjoyed." Lewis describes exactly what this sense of longing in the individual feels like, stating that it is

> an unsatisfied desire which is itself more desirable than any other satisfaction. I call it Joy, which is here a technical term and must be sharply distinguished both from Happiness and from Pleasure. Joy (in my sense) has indeed one characteristic, and one only, in common with them; the fact that anyone who has experienced it will want it again. Apart from that . . . it might almost equally well be called a particular kind of unhappiness or grief. But then it is a kind we want. I doubt whether anyone who has tasted it would ever, if both were in his power, exchange it for all the pleasures in the world.[11]

Lewis points out the tension in human longing, that we are, at the same moment, pained by its presence and yet inspired and invited by its reality. Lewis realized that the longing in him was "merely the mental track left by the passage of Joy—not the wave, but the wave's imprint on the sand." He had made an object of his longing of Joy, not acknowledging that "a desire is turned not to itself but to its object." Lewis's conversion began with his realization that there is an object that creates longing in humanity, an object that imprints Joy. Lewis speaks of this acknowledgment, saying

---

11. Lewis, *Surprised by Joy*, 17–18.

> This brought me into the region of awe, for I thus understood that in deepest solitude there is a road right out of the self, a commerce with something which, by refusing to identify itself with any object of the senses, or anything whereof we have biological or social need, or anything imagined, or any state of our own minds, proclaims itself sheerly objective. Far more objective than bodies, for it is not, like them, clothed in our senses; the naked Other, imageless (though our imagination salutes it with a hundred images) unknown, undefined, desired.[12]

Recognition of the object of human need was a step toward conversion for Lewis. His "awe" came from considering that Joy pointed toward something real—more real in fact, than Joy itself; an object for which the potency of Joy was only a prelude. Lewis entered this "region of awe" not by looking "at" his longing, but by looking "along" it to consider its meaning and origin. Looking "along" the supernatural not only reveals its reality, but such a perspective also the sheds light on the nature of the human. Lewis describes a radical change in his self-consciousness as a result of looking "along" the supernatural by trying to act in accordance with the divine will.

> You must not do, you must not even try to do, the will of the Father unless you are prepared. . . . All my acts, desires, and thoughts were to be brought into harmony with universal Spirit. For the first time I examined myself with a purely practical purpose. And there I found what appalled me; a zoo of lusts, a bedlam of ambitions, a nursery of fears, a hareem of fondled hatreds.[13]

Looking "along" the divine will causes an awakening as to the nature of the human. It is a perspective that sees the human for what he is, and considers what he can and needs to be. Conversion involves seeing what the divine sees when it considers humanity. This borrowed vision is the role of the imagination in the conversion process. In this way, the individual becomes aware of his

---

12. Lewis, *Surprised by Joy*, 221.
13. Lewis, *Surprised by Joy*, 226.

"But Only Say the Word, And I Shall Be Healed"

potential and his limitations. In order to act, the individual must become conscious of his options. Looking along the divine, which, as Lewis argues, includes attempting to see one's self from the divine perspective, paints an image of a potential lifestyle and disposition that the human can then act to bring about. Lewis examines the Lord's Prayer and the way in which it allows an individual to assume the divine perspective and bring into focus the divine will, which once apprehended, can be enacted. Lewis presents the prayer, saying:

> The very first words are *Our Father*. Do you now see what those words mean? They mean quite frankly, that you are putting yourself in the place of a son of God. . . . Why? What is the good of pretending to be what you are not? Well, even on the human level . . . there are two kinds of pretending. There is a bad kind, where the pretence is there instead of the real thing. . . . But there is also a good kind, where the pretence leads up to the real thing. . . . [V]ery often the best way to get a quality in reality is to start behaving as if you had it already.[14]

Lewis argues that when an individual "pretends," or dares to look "along" the divine will, "it is extremely likely that [he] will see at once some way in which at that very moment the pretense could be made less of a pretense and more of a reality."[15] "Contemplating" the divine is a thought process; "enjoying" it is an experience that can alter, permanently, one's philosophy, because it invites radically different images. One has only to think of the difference between contemplating and enjoying a friend; one is an intellectual consideration; the latter is a dialectic in which the other individual is known through the dynamic of a relationship. To contemplate a friend involves collecting and considering visual images of their appearance or other sensory perceptions, such as the sound of their voice or smell of their perfume or cologne. Contemplating a friend also involves distance; it is a purely intellectual exercise of considering the events or aspects of their life. Enjoying a friend

---

14. Lewis, *Mere Christianity*, 147.
15 Lewis, *Mere Christianity*, 148 ?

is to investigate their face to see, as well as to feel, their emotions; to allow the sound of their voice to remind you of past experience with them or others; or to close your eyes and allow the smell of their perfume or cologne to give proof of their presence without sight. Enjoying a friend is entering into a relationship where one seeks to know and be known beyond the sum of appearances, noises or smells. To enjoy a friendship is to share, even to bask, in the subjectivity of one another. This is precisely why conversion involves enjoying, for in conversion the human reaches out to the divine with a desire that the divine reach back; to know the divine beyond its face in the moral law, and to be known as a person beyond the sum total of actions in accord or in discord with that law. The freedom of the human will is not compromised or negated in this altered self-consciousness of enjoying; rather it is by choice that one opens himself to seek a relationship with the divine—personified in a will—beyond his own. The human will is challenged to forfeit solitude, not freedom. For those who are in the process of enjoying, rather than merely contemplating the divine,

> [t]heir free will is trembling inside them like the needle of a compass. But this is a needle that can choose.... Will the needle swing round, and settle, and point to God? He can help it to do so. He cannot force it. He cannot, so to speak, put out His own hand and pull it into the right position, for then it would not be free will anymore.[16]

Lewis defines his notion of the divine design for the relationship between humanity and God in his assertion of the voluntary presence of man in the relationship.

> The happiness which God designs for his creatures is the happiness of being freely, voluntarily united to Him and to each other in an ecstasy of love and delight compared with which the most rapturous love between a man and a woman on this earth is mere milk and water.[17]

---

16. Lewis, *Mere Christianity*, 164–65.
17. Lewis, *Mere Christianity*, 37–38.

"But Only Say the Word, And I Shall Be Healed"

The human will holds the power to choose, one might say to dare, to look "along" the supernatural. And it is the imagination that brings the human toward a synthesis of the contemplated and the enjoyed.

Lewis's fiction is essential for understanding his view of the relationship between the human and the divine, but fiction also allows the reader, in Lewis's terminology, to look along this interaction. In a unique way, fiction allows the reader to be a part of the religious experiences of the characters. Through fiction, Lewis offers the reader an opportunity to enjoy religious experience in way that mere contemplation does not allow.

Conversion, when it occurs in Narnia, is always a result of the individual's choice to seek a fulfillment for their sense of need in the character of Aslan. Not all characters are aware of who Aslan is when they first meet him. It is always a result of Aslan's will that these individuals meet him, but in two cases, we see the moment of conversion to the sufficiency of his will brought about by the desire of the individuals to accept and trust Aslan. One conversion involves a child who has taken off with a friend into a forest near their school. In showing off near a cliff, the girl's carelessness results in her friend's falling off the cliff. A Lion appears to save him, but then the boy and Lion disappear. Unsure of what has happened, and aware of her fault in the boy's accident, she begins to cry. After a long cry, she is tired and thirsty. She becomes aware of the sound of running water near her and sets out to find it.[18] The girl has never met Aslan before, and at the moment she sees him by the water, she becomes full of fear.[19] But the child drinks the water, the most refreshing she has ever tasted. And from that moment, she begins to confess her faults to the Lion, who accepts her confession and forgives her. At that point, she begins a relationship with Aslan that carries her into the land of Narnia. He tells her that he has a plan for life and for her service of him. The will of Aslan that the girl come to him to drink is unmistakable, and it dominates the young girl's experience of the Lion. Every servant of Aslan is faced

18. Lewis, *Silver Chair*, 17–19.
19. Lewis, *Silver Chair*, 63.

with this reality: that life, depicted in this passage as water without which Jill would die, flows from Aslan. This is the fact that is forced upon all those who encounter him. And yet, in the midst of Aslan's design that Jill see him save her friend and that she encounter him at the fountain, the young girl is set with the choice of whether to trust the Lion to allow her to drink. In this scene Lewis upholds his notion that the freedom of humanity is constant, fixed, and will never be tampered with by the divine. Lewis sees humanity as having a radical freedom. It is a freedom that allows for the possibility that humanity remain "thirsty"—here a metaphor for remaining independent of the divine—even to death. But when the child does surrender to Aslan, she immediately experiences a less stern face on the Lion. Her thoughts of fear from contemplating the Lion are transformed by her experience and enjoyment of him into a relationship of trust and love.

As Lewis states, conversion "is the change from being confident about our own efforts to the state in which we despair of doing anything for ourselves and leave it to God."[20] When Jill had finished drinking, the Lion told her to come to him. And Lewis adds that Jill knew she had to. The divine will in Narnia, when it is apprehended by humans, does not negate their freedom, but rather establishes unconditionally the only state of its fruition: harmony with the divine will. Lewis argues that the reality of the divine in the natural world is experienced as "objective value, the belief that certain attitudes are really true, and others really false, to the kinds of thing the universe is and the kind of things we are."[21] It is an objectivity that "*demands* a certain response from us whether we make it or not." Demand is experienced not as incarceration but as compulsion. Lewis says of his own conversion, that God's compulsion was his liberation.[22] The humans in the chronicles become aware of the reality of the divine will when they encounter Aslan. Those who freely choose to accept him experience conversion. The outcome rests with the free human response.

20. Lewis, *Mere Christianity*, 146.
21. Lewis, *Abolition of Man*, 18.
22. Lewis, *Surprised by Joy*, 280.

"But Only Say the Word, And I Shall Be Healed"

Fiction allows the reader to enjoy the possibility of conversion and even to feel the itch of their own scales, or the dryness of their own throat. The process of striving to unify sensory experience and intellectual or speculative postulation strives to identify meaning and reality. The imagination is the faculty that allows reason and intellect, volition and desire, a hypothetical ground to consider the possibilities for the employment of the individual will. In this way, the imagination is a workbench for the will. No one lacking in imagination has ever converted—or sinned.

Bibliography

Alexander, S. *Space, Time, and Deity: The Gifford Lectures at Glasgow, 1916–1918*. 2 vols. London: Macmillan, 1966.

Lewis, C. S. *The Abolition of Man*. New York: HarperOne, 1943.

———. "Meditation in a Toolshed." In *God in the Dock: Essays on Theology and Ethics*, edited by Walter Hooper, 230–35. Grand Rapids: Eerdmans, 1970.

———. *Mere Christianity*. New York: HarperOne, 1952.

———. *The Silver Chair*. New York: HarperCollins, 1953.

———. *Surprised by Joy: The Shape of My Early Life*. New York: HarperOne, 1955.

———. *"The Weight of Glory" and Other Addresses*. New York: HarperOne, 1949.

5

C. S. Lewis, Natural Theology, and Anglicanism

Ian S. Markham

IDENTIFYING THE "DEFINING CHARACTERISTICS" of a tradition is difficult. Often the framing of the question reflects vantage point. To identify, for example, the entrepreneurial spirit as a defining characteristic of America (which is often done) is a judgment made by those who are more fortunate in America rather than those who have been more disadvantaged by the American system. Yet when a certain people share a narrative and identify with a tradition, it is helpful to have some sense of what we share.

I take the view that the best way to think of "defining characteristics" of a tradition is not to search for something that everyone who self-identifies with the tradition would affirm—this is impossible to achieve—but instead to have some sense of what Ludwig Wittgenstein called "family resemblances."[1] In the case of Anglicanism, it is not that every Anglican would identify this or that as a "defining characteristic" of our tradition, but that it is a thread of a rope that connects our tradition together, which is shared by many within that tradition.

With this understanding of characteristics, we are now ready to explore natural theology. Unlike our Reformed friends,

1. Raatzsch, "*Philosophical Investigations* 65ff."

Anglicans have believed that there are certain assertions that we can make about God that do not depend on revelation. Anglicans have tended to believe that knowledge of God (whether God's existence or God's attributes or even God's action) can be found in areas beyond the witness of Scripture. Anglicans are nervous about a theology where sin is so overwhelming that even our human reason is distorted. Anglicans, on the whole, do not believe that we are so utterly depraved that we need the redeeming power of Christ before we can do anything good or anything right. These are the assumptions that make possible "natural theology."

The reason for our sympathy with natural theology is that our Reformation was never completely anti–Roman Catholic. King Henry VIII was honored with the title "Defender of the Faith" because he took issue with Martin Luther's views on the sacraments. The Book of Common Prayer owes much to our Catholic heritage. Our break with Rome was more pragmatic. An unbroken apostolic succession mattered; our view of the sacraments remained elevated; and therefore, the insight of Thomas Aquinas that knowledge of God was possible apart from revelation remained central.

Both English scientists and philosophers have seen the blending of insights from the natural world with our knowledge of God. We have Robert Boyle, in the seventeenth century, who advocated a "physico-theology"; Isaac Newton wrote *The Mathematical Principles of Natural Philosophy*; William Paley's *Natural Theology* remains a key text for the design argument; and Joseph Butler wrote *The Analogy of Religion, Natural and Revealed, to the Constitution and Course of Nature*. Anglicanism is shaped by a characteristic that involves the affirmation of natural theology.

Defining Natural Theology

It is Thomas Aquinas who is normally credited with the distinction between natural theology and revealed theology. Natural theology so understood involves the following commitments:

1. A recognition that the human mind is able to reason appropriately about the divine. Unlike Martin Luther, who took the view that the fall has made reason unreliable, Aquinas believed that the *imago Dei* safeguards reason sufficiently to still think, albeit in limited ways, about the divine. This means that the anthropology of Aquinas is a mediating position between the extremes of depravity (at one end) and liberal secular optimism (at the other). The *imago Dei* safeguards the capacity to reason; the fall means that we have propensities to sin.

2. The human mind, when used aright, is able to formulate reasons for the existence of God and the attributes of God. For Aquinas, this was the famous five ways. And from the corollary of each of those ways, the human mind can also work out that God's fundamental attributes include timelessness and necessary existence. There are reasons to think both that the arguments—the five ways—are not necessarily the strongest arguments and that the concept of God is not necessarily the most appropriate account of God. However, one can challenge some of the details of Aquinas's theology while affirming the insight that the human mind is still able to do this work.

With these two commitments, we will now embark on an examination of the work of C. S. Lewis in respect to natural theology.

C. S. Lewis and Arguments for Faith

It is clear that reason played a key and important role in the conversion of Lewis to Christianity. In *Surprised by Joy*, he writes about his horror when his close friend Barfield became an anthroposophist. Although he never joined Barfield as an anthroposophist, he does credit Barfield with a counterattack that demolished two assumptions. He writes:

> In the first place he made short work of what I have called my "chronological snobbery," the uncritical acceptance

of the intellectual climate common to our own age and the assumption that whatever has gone out of date is on that account discredited. You must find why it went out of date. Was it ever refuted (and if so by whom, where, and how conclusively) or did it merely die away as fashions do? If the latter, this tells us nothing about its truth or falsehood. From seeing this, one passes to the realisation that our own age is also "a period," and certainly has, like all periods, its own characteristic illusions.... In the second place he convinced me that the positions we had hitherto held left no room for any satisfactory theory of knowledge. We had been, in the technical sense of the term, "realists"; that is, we accepted as rock-bottom reality the universe revealed by the senses. But at the same time we continued to make for certain phenomena of consciousness all the claims that really went with a theistic or idealistic view. We maintained that abstract thought (if obedient to logical rules) gave indisputable truth, that our moral judgment was "valid," and our aesthetic experience not merely pleasing but "valuable." . . . Barfield convinced me that it was inconsistent. If thought were a purely subjective event, these claims for it would have to be abandoned. If one kept (as rock-bottom reality) the universe of the senses, aided by instruments and co-ordinated so as to form "science," then one would have to go much further—as many have since gone—and adopt a [b]ehaviouristic theory of logic, ethics, and aesthetics. But such a theory was, and is, unbelievable to me. I am using the word "unbelievable," which many use to mean "improbable" or even "undesirable," in a quite literal sense. I mean that the act of believing what the behaviourist believes is one that my mind simply will not perform. I cannot force my thought into that shape any more than I can scratch my ear with my big toe or pour wine out of a bottle into the cavity at the base of that same bottle. It is as final as a physical impossibility. I was therefore compelled to give up realism. . . . But now, it seemed to me, I had to give that up. Unless I were to accept an unbelievable alternative, I must admit that mind was no late-come epiphenomenon; that the whole universe was, in the last resort, mental; that our logic was participation in a cosmic *Logos*.[2]

It is interesting how the irrationality of naturalism, flowed into a commitment to idealism, which then led to a close reading of G. K. Chesterton's *Everlasting Man*, which then was followed by the religious experience. Lewis was "going up Headington Hill on the top of a bus."[3] It was then Lewis unbuckled himself and opened himself up to the experience of the divine.

Natural theology, therefore, is important to Lewis. For his own conversion, reason prepared the ground for the possibility of experience. The checkmate was made possible by his awareness that naturalism was utterly implausible. And it is in his engagement with naturalism that we find the two most substantial contributions from Lewis to natural theology.

The Argument from Reason

One irony embedded in the history of ideas is that it was Frederick Nietzsche who identified a major problem with naturalism (for which for the purposes of this paper, I am following Lewis's meaning—a worldview that believes the material world is all there is). How is reason possible? How can one affirm truth if all we are is a random result of a bundle of atoms? The case can be made that Nietzsche's enthusiasm for truth as projection on to the world is a corollary of Nietzsche's thinking through his atheism (and of course "thinking through" is ironic).[4] In addition, the argument from truth to the existence of God has a long and proud heritage. You can find it in Augustine and in Anselm. Interestingly, perhaps for reasons of accessibility, Lewis does not document the history of the argument.

Instead, he makes the case that reason needs God. His argument can be summarized thus: the genesis of reasoning cannot

---

2. Lewis, *Surprised by Joy*, 167–68.
3. Lewis, *Surprised by Joy*, 179.
4. Markham, *Truth and the Reality*, ch. 5.

simply be a physical interaction of brain events. Or as Lewis puts it:

> All possible knowledge, then, depends on the validity of reasoning. If the feeling of certainty which we express by words like *must be* and *therefore* and *since* is a real perception of how things outside our own minds really "must" be, well and good. But if this certainty is merely a feeling *in* our own minds and not a genuine insight into realities beyond them—if it merely represents the way our minds happen to work—then we can have no knowledge. Unless human reasoning is valid no science can be true.[5]

The point is simple. Why trust reason given it is simply a result of natural processes? Why is a conclusion right if all that is happening is blind physical processes are just blending together to create the answer? The genesis of the mind, which of course for a naturalist is nothing more than the processes of the physical brain, makes trusting the conclusions of the mind difficult. Analogies at this point might be helpful to understand Lewis. So, let me try my own: If you find one day, outside the seminary on Seminary Road, the wind has blown a garbage bin over and created what looks to you as a pattern spelling the word "dinosaur," would you not conclude, assuming that you are sure that the wind is the only force responsible for scattered garbage, that the garbage clearly is not spelling the word "dinosaur"? Winds do not spell words. Words require a person with agency and intention. A random process cannot be trusted to point to truth. Indeed, if it does look like the word "dinosaur" is written by the garbage on the road, one is much more likely to assume that a person has clearly taken the rubbish and decided to write the word. Reasoning reflects intention, which argues Lewis, stands outside the material processes.

Charles Taliaferro's discussion of this argument concludes that Lewis has overstated his case. Although the argument might work against strict naturalism (a naturalism that "see[s] nature as, ultimately, that which may be described and explained in terms

---

5. Lewis, *Miracles*, 18–19.

of a complete physics"[6]). But it is less effective against broad naturalists who "allow for the emergence of consciousness among humans and some non-human animals."[7] Taliaferro is also worried that Lewis has overstated his argument that, of necessity, mind requires the claim that there is something transcending the material that makes mind possible. In short, Taliaferro is feeling that a broad naturalist could claim that somehow in the processes of nature a configuration of the material could create mind that then would have a distinctive impact in terms of reasoning and agency.

While it might be true that some way can be found to reconcile naturalism with the emergence of mind, one must concede that Lewis is on terrain that is strong for theism. There is a mystery about mind. It is puzzling that mind cannot be located in the brain, and certainly the sheer range of mental life (from memory to fantasy to complex arguments) cannot be detected by any machine examining the processes of the brain. Lewis is inviting the reader to think about the fundamentals of life. The person reading is a thinking reality. But what does thought suggest about the nature of the universe?

My own argument from truth to God rested on the assumption that truth assumes a universe that is stable and consistent. Truth implies that the universe is intelligible. Intelligibility assumes a universe that is not random or potentially chaotic. If something is the case (namely, it is true), then the assertion invites a sense of confidence. We need divine agency to make sense of our assumptions about truth.

With Lewis, the invitation for the atheist is to think through the following: Exactly what I am assuming when I reason? What sort of universe gives me confidence in my capacity to reach a rational conclusion in say science? In my reading, Lewis is of the view that most atheists are really anonymous theists. With the possible exception of Nietzsche, most atheists live like theists. They trust their capacity to reason more than their assumptions about the nature of the universe would permit them to do so.

6. Taliaferro, "Naturalism," 105.

7. Taliaferro, "Naturalism," 105.

This is a good segue to the second and more famous of his arguments for the existence of God—the argument from morality.

The Argument from Morality

It is at the start of *Mere Christianity* that Lewis outlines his argument from morality. The opening chapter is worth quoting at length:

> Every one has heard people quarrelling. Sometimes it sounds funny and sometimes it sounds merely unpleasant; but however it sounds, I believe we can learn something very important from listening to the kind of things they say. They say things like this: "How'd you like it if anyone did the same to you?"—"That's my seat, I was there first"—"Leave him alone, he isn't doing you any harm"—"Why should you shove in first?"—"Give me a bit of your orange, I gave you a bit of mine"—"Come on, you promised." People say things like that every day, educated people as well as uneducated, and children as well as grown-ups. Now what interests me about all these remarks is that the man who makes them is not merely saying that the other man's behaviour does not happen to please him. He is appealing to some kind of standard of behaviour which he expects the other man to know about. And the other man very seldom replies: "To hell with your standard." Nearly always he tries to make out that what he has been doing does not really go against the standard, or that if it does there is some special excuse. He pretends there is some special reason in this particular case why the person who took the seat first should not keep it, or that things were quite different when he was given the bit of orange, or that something has turned up which lets him off keeping his promise. It looks, in fact, very much as if both parties had in mind some kind of Law or Rule of fair play or decent behaviour or morality or whatever you like to call it, about which they really agreed. And they have. If they had not, they might, of course, fight like animals, but they could not quarrel in the human sense of the word. Quarrelling

means trying to show that the other man is in the wrong. And there would be no sense in trying to do that unless you and he had some sort of agreement as to what Right and Wrong are; just as there would be no sense in saying that a footballer had committed a foul unless there was some agreement about the rules of football. Now this Law or Rule about Right and Wrong used to be called the Law of Nature.[8]

The title of this chapter is "The Law of Human Nature." It is an elegant piece of writing that makes accessible a profound issue. How do we make sense of our moral discourse? Embedded in our moral discourse, points out Lewis, is an assumption that the claims of morality transcend human communities. The word "ought" seems to imply a standard outside human life that is putting pressure on us to behave in a certain way. The word "ought" is never the same as the word "desire" or "like." If I say, "I really ought to go and visit my sick friend in hospital," then the implication is that "although I would prefer to go to the pub with you and have a drink, I really ought to do otherwise." My own preferences are to go for a drink, but the moral obligation is putting pressure on me to do otherwise.

Having raised the puzzle, Lewis needs now to link the language of morality with God. So, he takes the following steps. First, he stresses the remarkable phenomenon of basic moral values being universal. In *The Abolition of Man*, he uses the Chinese concept of "the Tao":

> The Chinese also speak of a great thing (the greatest thing) called the *Tao*. . . . It is Nature, it is the Way, the Road. It is the Way in which the universe goes on, the Way in which things everlastingly emerge, stilly and tranquilly, into space and time. . . . This conception in all its forms, Platonic, Aristotelian, Stoic, Christian, and Oriental alike, I shall henceforth refer to for brevity simply as "the *Tao*." Some of the accounts of it which I have quoted will seem, perhaps, to many of you merely quaint or even magical. But what is common to them all is something we cannot neglect. It is the doctrine of

8. Lewis, *Mere Christianity*, 3–4.

> objective value, the belief that certain attitudes are really true, and others really false, to the kind of thing the universe is and the kind of things we are. Those who know the *Tao* can hold that to call children delightful or old men venerable is not simply to record a psychological fact about our own parental or filial emotions at the moment, but to recognize a quality which *demands* a certain response from us whether we make it or not.[9]

Although he concedes that there are different moral codes in different cultures (some Muslims permit polygamy while Christians have to be monogamous), the underlying precepts are universal (love your neighbor, the Golden Rule, venerate the elderly). And when a culture decides to embark on acts of evil, for example, the Nazis in Germany against the Jewish people, Lewis insists that deep down those involved in these acts knew they were wrong.

The second step is to suggest that the religious explanation for this fundamental moral unity is stronger than the naturalist explanation. He frames the two options in the following way:

> And, very roughly, two views have been held. First, there is what is called the materialist view. People who take that view think that matter and space just happen to exist, and always have existed, nobody knows why; and that the matter, behaving in certain fixed ways, has just happened, by a sort of fluke, to produce creatures like ourselves who are able to think. By one chance in a thousand something hit our sun and made it produce the planets; and by another thousandth chance the chemicals necessary for life, and the right temperature, occurred on one of these planets, and so some of the matter on this earth came alive; and then, by a very long series of chances, the living creatures developed into things like us. The other view is the religious view. According to it, what is behind the universe is more like a mind than it is like anything else we know. That is to say, it is conscious, and has purposes, and prefers one thing to another. And on this view it made the universe, partly for purposes we do not know, but partly, at any rate, in order to produce

---

9. Lewis, *Abolition of Man*, 8–9.

creatures like itself—I mean, like itself to the extent of having minds.[10]

For Lewis, the religious explanation makes most sense because as a person examines their experience of the moral law, it is an experience that seems more likely to have come from a mind than from matter. Our human experience of the moral law is analogous to receiving instructions. We are feeling told to behave in certain ways. Minds can give instructions; matter cannot. Therefore, a cosmic mind is more likely to make sense of morality than morality simply being an accident of nature.

As Taliaferro notes Lewis does not actually develop a theory of precisely how God shares the moral instructions with humanity. Taliaferro suggests that Lewis's sympathies are with a divine command theory of the ethical. This runs into the classic problem of Plato's Euthyphro dilemma: "Is the pious loved by the gods because it is pious, or is it pious because it is loved by the gods?"[11] Or to update the language underpinning the conundrum: Does God command the good, which therefore means the good in some sense transcends God; or is whatever God chooses to command the good, which means the good could be arbitrary?

Following Aquinas and others, I tend to the view that the most helpful way to frame the location of the ethical is in the character of God. Given God is a necessary being, God is not capricious. God is Love; God is the Good; God is the source of the law of nature. In God's very Being, the moral values of the universe are located.

Both the argument from reason and the argument from morality have some force. Lewis is inviting the reader to reflect on their experience. The reader is "thinking"; the reader is "reasoning." Do you really think that the capacity to reason and reach conclusion is a result ultimately of matter? Or do you think that a much more plausible explanation is a cosmic mind? Like gives birth to like. Alternatively, argues Lewis, how do you make sense of

---

10. Lewis, *Mere Christianity*, 30–31.
11. Plato, *Dialogues*, 14.

the innate instruction manual that humanity has been given across all cultures in the world. Minds give instructions, not inanimate matter. What is interesting in the framing of these arguments is the centrality of mind in the argument. Underpinning the apologetics of Lewis is, in the end, idealism.

The Centrality of Idealism for Lewis

Alistair McGrath has helpfully identified the importance of "Oxford realism" for the formation of Lewis. This Oxford realism highlights the centrality of matter which is known by the senses. The first step is innocent enough: knowledge is discovery; it is, writes McGrath, "independent of the act of knowing."[12] The second step is more contentious: the primary vehicle of knowing is the five senses. What we see, touch, taste, hear, and smell is it. Now we run into the problem of morality and aesthetics. Lewis wanted to safeguard the objectivity of moral value and beauty. So, writes McGrath:

> By about 1923, Lewis was in the process of moving away from "Oxford Realism" to embrace a form of "Absolute Idealism." He retained his belief in a universe revealed by the senses. However, he came to realize that his affirmation of a nature that was "quite independent of our observation," "something other" than ourselves, demanded a greater vision of reality, which extended to the way in which we think and reason. Lewis came to the conclusion . . . that there was some "first principle" embedded within the universe and human reason, that enabled it to reason aright, in conformity with a deeper vision of reality.[13]

McGrath is right: the idealism of Lewis was a crucial step in his gradual conversion to Christianity. So, in conclusion, let us reflect on the importance of idealism.

---

12. McGrath, *Intellectual World*, 37.
13. McGrath, *Intellectual World*, 39.

In the argument between mind and matter, Christians, in the end, have to give primacy to mind. After all, it is God—the mind at the heart of all things—who creates the material world. And if the material world is all there is, then God does not exist. Persuading skeptics of the primacy of mind is hard. After all, matter is obvious. However, it is interesting that science is increasingly sympathetic to forms of idealism than to forms of materialism.[14]

It is Keith Ward who has made this a central theme of his work. Unlike some idealists, he does not take the view that everything that exists is consciousness or mind, but instead "material things could not exist without a mental basis." He suggest three steps that can get a person to idealism. He writes: "The first step towards Idealism is to see that without sense-perceptions (awareness of colors, smells, tastes, and touches) we would have no knowledge at all. Without feelings, we could not distinguish between good and bad experiences. Without thoughts, we could not make sense of our perceptions by thinking of them as perceptions of external objects. Without intentions, we could not actively explore. And understand our environment."[15] Mind does the hard work of creating experiences.

Ward's second step is to recognize that these perceptions, thoughts, and feelings cannot be considered as the same or reducible to certain material qualities (Ward is thinking of mass, spatial location here). There is no way that thoughts are the same as the electricity activity and blood flows of the brain. It is here that he cites our current scientific worldview. Ward writes:

> In modern physics, colors like green or tastes like sweetness are not properties which exist apart from our perception of them. I see a green patch; it exists. But a physicist will point out that what is happening is that a certain wavelength of light hits the retina, and is turned into electrical signals to various parts of the brain, which then generate the sensation of greenness. The sensation is very different from the objective wavelength. The same

---

14. Lewis, *Miracles*, 19–28.
15. Ward, *Personal Idealism*, 17.

sort of thing is true of all our perceptions. What we perceive (colored solid three dimensional objects) does not exist when it is not being observed. Without observations the physical properties of the world, according to physics, are entities like force-fields or probabilistic wave-forms, perhaps in eleven dimensions, which we never perceive as they are. If so, the world we perceive is a function of our consciousness, not what exists in an unobserved physical world.[16]

His third and final step is to recognize the nature of this world. It isn't that there are two distinctive worlds, which are mysteriously connected. Instead, he writes: "Conscious experience is the fundamental reality." The actual experience of green is more real than the actual construct of physics. He does stress that "of course, there is an external reality which gives rise to our experiences. But that reality too is composed of consciousness."[17] After all, God is the divine mind who creates the external reality.

Standing Back

The goal of this chapter is twofold. First, I wanted to show that Lewis outlines an apologetic that is powerful and important. Grounded in idealism, he demonstrates how the most fundamental features of our humanity need the divine explanation. Our capacity to reason and our capacity to be morally aware are deep mysteries that are made possible by the truth that we are created by a cosmic mind underpinning everything that is. Most atheists are, in truth, anonymous theists. Most trust their capacity to reason; most take seriously certain moral obligations. And these ways of thinking and living point to the reality of God. Second, I wanted to affirm that Lewis is an Anglican. The Episcopal Church and the Anglican Communion need to reclaim Lewis. His commitment to natural theology—to the very possibility of arriving at reasons for faith—is an Anglican commitment. We do not invite the seeker

16. Ward, *Personal Idealism*, 18.
17. Ward, *Personal Idealism*, 18.

to a leap of faith or advocate a blind faith. Instead, we invite the seeker to use their minds as they make sense of living and life. And in so doing to find faith in all its richness.

Bibliography

Lewis, C. S. *The Abolition of Man*. New York: HarperOne, 1943.
———. *Miracles*. New York: HarperOne, 1947.
———. *Surprised by Joy: The Shape of My Early Life*. New York: HarperOne, 1955.
Markham, Ian. *Truth and the Reality of God: An Essay in Natural Theology*. Edinburgh: T&T Clark, 1998.
McGrath, Alister E. *The Intellectual World of C. S. Lewis*. Malden, MA: Wiley Blackwell, 2014.
Plato. *Five Dialogues: Euthyphro, Apology, Crito, Meno, Phaedo*. Translated by G. M. A. Grube. Revised by John M. Cooper. 2nd ed. Hackett Classics. Indianapolis: Hackett, 2002.
Raatzsch, Richard. "*Philosophical Investigations* 65ff: On Family Resemblance." Wittgenstein Archives at the University of Bergen, n.d. https://wab.uib.no/agora/tools/wab/collection-3-issue-1-article-4.annotate.
Taliaferro, Charles. "On Naturalism." In *The Cambridge Companion to C. S. Lewis*, edited by Robert MacSwain and Michael Ward, 105–19. Cambridge Companions to Religion. Cambridge: Cambridge University Press, 2010.
Ward, Keith. *Personal Idealism*. My Theology 13. London: Darton, Longman, and Todd, 2022.

6

"Oh Unless It Were You"
C. S. Lewis and the Poetry of Friendship

KAREN SWALLOW PRIOR

TO WRITE ABOUT C. S. Lewis and friendship is akin to writing about C. S. Lewis and literature. Or C. S. Lewis and life. Or C. S. Lewis and air.

From Philip and Carol Zaleski to Alan Jacobs to Alister McGrath to nearly every biographer and critic in between, those who have studied the life of C. S. Lewis describe him as a person for whom friendship meant more than almost all else. Friendships fueled his literary works, formed the foundation of his marriage, and became the path to the Christian faith he embraced as an adult. Lewis wrote about friendship in his poetry, his stories, and devoted a chapter to it in one of his most famous works, *The Four Loves*.

So perhaps I will make this attempt by starting with C. S. Lewis and death. Not any death, but the death of his friend, the poem he wrote about that death and that friendship, and the glimpse these lines offer into the many words Lewis offered on friendship.

Originally titled "On the Death of Charles Williams," this poem was first published in *Britain Today* in August of 1945, just a few months after Williams's death. Lewis later changed the title to the one used in his collection, *Poems*: "To Charles Williams."[1]

---

1. Kawano, "Impact of Charles Williams' Death."

The poem reads to us today not only as a tribute to the friendship and the loss of that friendship that occasioned the verse, but also as a narrow window into Lewis's experience of friendship. His views about friendship are, of course, clearly explicated in *The Four Loves*. But explanation is to experience as a recipe is to warm bread sliced and served. In this poem (among other of his works), Lewis's beliefs about friendship are made manifest as an embodied experience.

Central to embodied experience is sensory experience. Fittingly then, the poem opens by invoking the sense of sound. Sound is key to poetry, of course, which Lewis knew well and demonstrates powerfully here by employing the alliterative meter that characterizes the Anglo-Saxon and Old Norse poetry he so loved. In his essay "The Alliterative Metre," Lewis explains for modern readers accustomed to classical syllabic verse the ancient sounds of his linguistic forebears: "The thing to aim at is richness and fullness of sound."[2] Syllabic verse, Lewis writes, depends on the evocative qualities of words, but alliterative poetry evokes in phrases. In alliterative meter the phrase, rather than the line, "is the poetic unit."[3] And what is a phrase but a friendship of words?

Poetry and friendship are connected in how both depend on and reflect sensory experience. Indeed, current research on the brain reveals "the sensory nature of friendship—the central role of our vision, hearing, and touch in processing social information from the outside world and passing it on to higher-order brain areas."[4]

So read (or attend) to this poem with both ear and eye, hearing the repetition of the sounds not only mark the meter, but also tighten the phrasal bonds:

> Your death blows a strange bugle call, friend, and all is hard
> To see plainly or record truly. The new light imposes change,
> Re-adjusts all a life-landscape as it thrusts down its probe from
>   the sky,

2. Lewis, "Alliterative Metre," 128.
3. Lewis, "Alliterative Metre," 127.
4. Denworth, *Friendship*, 17.

> To create shadows, to reveal waters, to erect hills and deepen
> glens.
> The slant alters. I can't see the old contours. It's a larger world
> Than I once thought it. I wince, caught in the bleak air that
> blows on the ridge.
> Is it the first sting of the great winter, the world-waning? Or
> the cold of spring?
> A hard question and worth talking a whole night on.
> But with whom? Of whom now can I ask guidance? With what
> friend concerning your death
> Is it worth while to exchange thoughts unless—oh unless it
> were you?[5]

Examining this poem, key image by key image, resonant phrase by resonant phrase, offers an embodied, sensory experience of some of the ways in which Lewis experienced friendship—and its loss.

"YOUR DEATH"

The poem begins by making clear that this is an apostrophe: it addresses an absent friend. The subject of this address is that absence. "Your death," the speaker says, in a direct address to the one who is no longer there, Charles Lewis.

Lewis's friendship with this novelist and Oxford University Press editor is famous and well documented, as are the other friendships that formed the literary circle known as the Inklings. Williams and Lewis had befriended one another initially through correspondence (each writing to the other mutual admiration for their work), but with the breakout of war in 1936, Williams was relocated from his London office to Oxford, where he was able to join the Inklings in their regular gatherings. Williams died on May 15, 1948, days after the end of the war, unexpectedly, a strange loss indeed.

---

5. "To Charles Williams," in Lewis, *Poems*, 164.

"BLOWS A STRANGE BUGLE CALL"

Thus, Williams's "death blows a strange bugle call," the speaker laments. The bugle, of course, is the instrument used on the battlefield or the war camp to call out instructions, the most famous of these being the "Taps" played at the end of the day—or, more poignantly, at the end of a life. Lewis, of course, knew firsthand the death that comes on the battlefield. The same shrapnel that wounded him in the trenches of France decades before during World War I had killed his dear friend Laurence Johnson. Johnson, who had been a budding scholar at Queen's College, is the friend who taught the young Lewis the joy of a camaraderie built on lively, good-natured debate over serious subjects as well as a shared commitment to duty, virtue, and the love of truth.[6] Indeed, even after the loss of this early friend, Lewis's deepest and longest friendships—whether with Williams, J. R. R. Tolkien, Owen Barfield, or Dorothy Sayers—were characterized by generous disagreement as much as shared values.

Lewis had heard many—likely far too many—bugle calls in his life. It is hard not to imagine that the hard traumas of that first war were not conjured for Lewis by this sudden metaphorical call of the bugle. Perhaps that is part of what made this one so "strange." Perhaps, too, it was that it was so unexpected, so seemingly far removed from the battlefield—although this death, too, occurred in the context of a world war, the second one, which had ended just days before Williams's death. Ironically, it was, as already mentioned, this later war that had brought Lewis and Williams into the close proximity that fostered the growth of their friendship and brought Williams into the circle of the Inklings. The Inklings were knit together primarily by their shared love of literature and literary discussions. Yet, there was more that cemented their bonds as the "joy of friendship and the company of the Inklings contrasted sharply with the realities of war, which made many demands and required sacrifice."[7]

---

6. Jacobs, *Narnian*, xx; McGrath, *Lunch with C. S. Lewis*, 89.
7. Duriez, *C. S. Lewis*, 177.

Writing, criticism, teaching, and cultivating community are their own types of work, and they also require certain kinds of sacrifices. And whether it was the work of war or the work of writing, Lewis's dearest friends developed their sense of community within the context of that work.

Alister McGrath, imagining himself having a lunch with Lewis, describes the role these friends and their communal work played in Lewis's life this way:

> Lewis was no solitary genius, who lived and worked in isolation. He needed friends to support and encourage him. He needed friends who could inspire him—to enable him to become a better person and a better writer. Some of Lewis's friends, such as Arthur Greeves, gave him emotional support; others, such as J. R. R. Tolkien, gave him intellectual encouragement. And Lewis's conversion—first to belief in God, and then to Christianity—owed an incalculable amount to his close friends such as Owen Barfield and Tolkien.[8]

It is "a good thing," Lewis observed, "that personal friendship should grow up between those who work together."[9] And he was careful to point out to Williams in 1942, "that, far from loving your work because you are my friend, I first sought your friendship because I loved your books"[10]—in other words, the work. The "strange bugle call" did not just sound the end of days for a dear friend, but it was a reminder of the work that had done been together and that would continue on despite the fall of a beloved comrade in arms.

"ALL IS HARD TO SEE PLAINLY OR RECORD TRULY"

For Lewis, part of the work of friendship—and its joy—was a shared pursuit and understanding of truth. This was the basis of his camaraderie with fellow soldier Laurence Johnson. It was the

---

8. McGrath, *Lunch with C. S. Lewis*, 18.
9. Lewis, "Inner Ring," 60.
10. Lewis, "Dedication."

foundation of his fiery sparring and fireside readings with his fellow Inklings. Their debates over various literary styles, themes, and authors (as well as religious beliefs) demonstrated nothing more than that in life, as in death, "all is hard to see plainly or record truly." But friends help us to see and say truth.

> Writing in *Surprised by Joy* about his friends Arthur Greeves and Own Barfield, Lewis explains how the varieties of friendships work their varieties of magic toward the same end: There is a sense in which Arthur and Barfield are the types of every man's First Friend and Second Friend. The First is the alter ego, the man who first reveals to you that you are not alone in the world by turning out (beyond hope) to share all your most secret delights. There is nothing to be overcome in making him your friend; he and you join like rain-drops on a window. But the Second Friend is the man who disagrees with you about everything. He is not so much the alter ego as the anti-self. Of course he shares your interests; otherwise he would not become your friend at all. But he has approached them all at a different angle.[11]

Iron sharpens iron, the Scriptures say in Prov 27:17. But there are different kinds of iron.

Even Lewis's primary academic friend, J. R. R. Tolkien, despite their intellectual agreements and interests, was quite different from Lewis in literary tastes as well as doctrinal beliefs. As Lewis describes it in *Surprised by Joy*, friendship with Tolkien "marked the breakdown of two old prejudices. At my first coming into the world I had been (implicitly) warned never to trust a Papist, and at my first coming [in 1925] into the English Faculty (explicitly) never to trust a philologist. Tolkien was both."[12]

Some friends (perhaps the best kinds) cultivate in us the desire for our own sharpening. In another of Lewis's poems, "To a Friend," which, significantly, appears in the collected *Poems* immediately before "To Charles Williams," Lewis envisions the fullness of knowledge that may come after earthly life, in eternity. If

---

11. Lewis, *Surprised by Joy*, 30.
12. Lewis, *Surprised by Joy*, 209.

knowledge can live on after death, the poem suggests, then this friend's knowledge will bear apples of gold, grow spices, and host tuneful birds in a green paradise—the fruit of earthly wisdom brought forth into everlasting life. But alas, Lewis laments, his own mind, in comparison to his friend's, will prove barren, bare, and rocky.[13]

If knowledge can live on after death, the poem suggests, than this friend's knowledge will bear apples of gold and host tuneful birds in a green paradise. But, alas, the speaker fears his own mind will prove barren, bare, and rocky.

Whether this speaker's low esteem of himself reflects Lewis's own self-doubts about his intellectual ability or not, we cannot know for certain. But we do know that Lewis found in friendship the opportunity to seek and find not only knowledge, but truth. As he writes in *The Four Loves*:

> For us of course the shared activity and therefore the companionship on which Friendship supervenes will not often be a bodily one like hunting or fighting. It may be a common religion, common studies, a common profession, even a common recreation. All who share it will be our companions; but one or two or three who share something more will be our Friends. In this kind of love, as Emerson said, Do you love me? means Do you see the same truth?—Or at least, "Do you care about the same truth?" The man who agrees with us that some question, little regarded by others, is of great importance can be our Friend. He need not agree with us about the answer.[14]

We also know, from the next poem in the collection, that with the death of another friend, Lewis's knowledge did indeed grow.

"THE SLANT ALTERS"

In a 1948 review of one of Williams's novels, newly published in the US, *Time* described Williams as "the contemporary from

---

13. "To a Friend," in Lewis, *Poems*, 163.
14. Lewis, *Four Loves*, 97.

whom [Lewis] had learned most."[15] Indeed, friendship, the poem to Williams suggests, is a kind of light. The light that friendship brings alters all that we see, and in altering what we see, what we know. "As long as we are thinking only of natural values," Lewis observed, "we must say that the sun looks down on nothing half so good as a household laughing together over a meal, or two friends talking over a pint of beer."[16]

The death of a friend is a shifting of the light, a lowering of the sun, a shifting of the ray. And it was Williams's death that brought one of the most profound alterations of what Lewis knew. The poem implies this effect, but in a letter, Lewis makes this even more explicit.

> You will have heard of the death of my dearest friend, Charles Williams and, no doubt, prayed for him. For me too, it has been, and is, a great loss. But not at all a dejecting one. It has greatly increased my faith. Death has done nothing to my idea of him, but he has done—oh, I can't say what—to my idea of death. It has made the next world much more real and palpable. We all feel the same. How one lives and learns. I have often heard of widows and bereaved mothers who "felt that 'he' was nearer now to them than while in the body" and always thought it sentimental hyperbole. I know better now.[17]

Even more starkly, in his *Preface to Essays Presented to Charles Williams*, published in 1947, Lewis wrote, "No event has so corroborated my faith in the next world as Williams did simply by dying. When the idea of death and the idea of Williams thus met in my mind, it was the idea of death that was changed."[18]

By the time of Williams's death, Lewis had long been a Christian. And yet his view of death—its defeat in Christ, one of the central doctrines of Christianity—took a new slant all those years later because of, not only the influence, but the death of a friend, a

---

15. *Time*, "Religion," final para.
16. Lewis, "Membership," 32.
17. Lewis, *Books, Broadcasts, and War*, 656.
18. Lewis, Preface, n.p.

death that brought that friend, in some way (spiritually, theologically, emotionally) nearer.

One can't help but contrast the image of this poem's slant of light, whose source was the light of friendship, with a similar image presented by Emily Dickinson. Yet, their similarity is accompanied by a stark difference in mood and tone, and likely not coincidentally because Dickinson's was a life was not characterized by the deep bonds of friendship that marked Lewis's life.

> There's a certain Slant of light,
> Winter Afternoons—
> That oppresses, like the Heft
> Of Cathedral Tunes—
> Heavenly Hurt, it gives us—
> We can find no scar,
> But internal difference—
> Where the Meanings, are—
> None may teach it—Any—
> 'Tis the seal Despair—
> An imperial affliction
> Sent us of the Air—[19]

"IT THRUSTS DOWN ITS PROBE FROM THE SKY"

Yet, like Lewis, Dickinson (whose work is not listed among the volumes in Lewis's personal library) connected light to truth in a way that reflects what Lewis shows about the new knowledge his friend's death brought him:

> Tell all the truth but tell it slant—
> Success in Circuit lies
> Too bright for our infirm Delight
> The Truth's superb surprise
> As Lightning to the Children eased
> With explanation kind
> The Truth must dazzle gradually
> Or every man be blind—[20]

19. Dickinson, "There's a Certain Slant."
20. Dickinson, "Tell the Truth."

This indirect (yet significant) power of light is exactly what C. S. Lewis is getting at in a famous essay from *God in the Dock*, a passage that contains some of his most beloved lines.

> I was standing today in the dark toolshed. The sun was shining outside and through the crack at the top of the door there came a sunbeam. From where I stood that beam of light, with the specks of dust floating in it, was the most striking thing in the place. Everything else was almost pitchblack. I was seeing the beam, not seeing things by it. Then I moved, so that the beam fell on my eyes. Instantly the whole previous picture vanished. I saw no toolshed, and (above all) no beam. Instead I saw, framed in the irregular cranny at the top of the door, green leaves moving on the branches of a tree outside and beyond that, 90 odd million miles away, the sun. Looking along the beam, and looking at the beam are very different experiences.[21]

And in another more famous line, taken from a paper delivered at Oxford, Lewis expands on this metaphor of light even more: "I believe in Christianity as I believe that the Sun has risen, not only because I see it, but because by it I see everything else."[22]

While the limited scope of this paper won't allow a thorough exploration of Lewis's frequent use of light imagery, we have enough here to trace some key connections. For Lewis, the sun and light allow him to see—really see—the world (an idea we will return to below). So too do friendships help him discover truth—also expressed in metaphors of light—in such a way that he can better see ultimate reality. "In each of my friends there is something only some other friend can fully bring out. By myself I am not large enough to call the whole man into activity; I want other lights than my own to show all his facets."[23]

---

21. Lewis, "Meditation in a Toolshed," 230.
22. Lewis, *Weight of Glory*, 139–40.
23. Lewis, *Four Loves*, 92.

"NEW LIGHT IMPOSES CHANGE"

Returning to Alister McGrath's imaginary lunch with Lewis, let us note one of McGrath's key observations: "So what might we conclude? Perhaps the most important point to take away from our lunch with Lewis is that friendship is of vital importance because friendship is transformational—both for ourselves and for our friends."[24]

The transformative power of friendship is central to Lewis's understanding (as well as his own experience). As he puts it in *The Four Loves*, "The little knots of Friends who turn their backs on the 'World' are those who really transform it."[25] Later, he adds, "Every real Friendship is a sort of secession, even a rebellion."[26] And we know that this wasn't theoretical knowledge. It was lived out by the Inklings. Alan Jacobs writes in *The Narnian* not only that Lewis was "a shrewd analyst of the countercultural possibilities of true friendship," but also that the Inklings "constituted a tiny counterculture."[27]

As noted already, "it was Lewis's friends, and not priests or pastors, that helped him convert to Christianity"[28]—the greatest transformation—the most radical counterrevolution—of all.

"TO CREATE SHADOWS, TO REVEAL WATERS, TO ERECT HILLS AND DEEPEN GLENS"

Friends don't just transform us. They form us. Friends add texture and depth to our external and internal worlds. These phrases from the poem literally denote the surfaces of the external world. Yet, metaphorically, these images speak to the depths of one's heart, mind, and soul that friendships are capable of mining in order to bring out the riches of human experience.

24. McGrath, *Lunch with C. S. Lewis*, 26.
25. Lewis, *Four Loves*, 101.
26. Lewis, *Four Loves*, 114.
27. Jacobs, *Narnian*, 203.
28. Apichella, "Friendship as Philosopher," 106.

These riches include the universals of the human condition, but they also include the particular gifts of individuality. As Lewis says, the "outlook which values the collective above the individual necessarily disparages Friendship; it is a relation between men at their highest level of individuality."[29] He continues,

> Hence true Friendship is the least jealous of loves. Two friends delight to be joined by a third, and three by a fourth, if only the newcomer is qualified to become a real friend. They can then say, as the blessed souls say in Dante, "Here comes one who will augment our loves." For in this love "to divide is not to take away."[30]

Of course, these universals and these particularities can be good, or they can be evil. Thus, as Lewis observes, friendship "can be a school of virtue" or "a school of vice." In this way, friendship "is ambivalent. It makes good men better and bad men worse."[31] It creates, reveals, erects, and deepens. For better or worse.

A significant part of Lewis's understanding of friendship is based on his belief that it is "the least natural of loves; the least instinctive, organic, biological, gregarious, and necessary" and that "we can live and breed without friendship."[32] Friendship, he goes on to say, "is unnecessary, like philosophy, like art, like the universe itself (for God did not need to create.) It has no survival value; rather it is one of those things which give value to survival."[33] Of course, Lewis was talking of mere biological necessity as it was understood at the time. Given Lewis's prescient and prophetic views on animal suffering and the connection of their pain to human suffering,[34] he would no doubt be unsurprised by current developments in cognitive science showing the necessity of social connections for biological life in the lives of many animal species. This science demonstrates that social connections forge

---

29. Lewis, *Four Loves*, 90.
30. Lewis, *Four Loves*, 92.
31. Lewis, *Four Loves*, 115.
32. Lewis, *Four Loves*, 88.
33. Lewis, *Four Loves*, 103.
34. Lewis, *Problem of Pain*, 133–43.

connections and pathways in the brain that affect every aspect of our lives, even our physical health. In her work collating a great deal of this research, *Friendship: The Evolution, Biology, and Extraordinary Power of Life's Fundamental Bond*, Lydia Denworth remarks, "All due respect to C. S. Lewis, but he was wrong."[35]

Denworth recounts in her book a vast body of research done on animals that offers evidence that, particularly for mammals, social networks are necessary, not only for thriving, but often for merely surviving. Friendship, Denworth shows, "actually is a matter of life and death." She explains, "It is carried in our DNA, in how we're wired. Social bonds have the power to shape the trajectories of our lives. And that means friendship is not a choice or a luxury; it's a necessity that is critical to our ability to succeed and thrive."[36]

Of course, Lewis wasn't wrong that friends aren't necessary to mere biological survival of individuals. Yet, he seems to instinctively understand that we do, in fact, need friends when he writes, "We live, in fact, in a world starved for solitude, silence, and privacy; and therefore starved for meditation and true friendship."[37] And he further observes the significance of this starvation in writing, "To the Ancients, Friendship seemed the happiest and most fully human of all loves; the crown of life and the school of virtue. The modern world, in comparison, ignores it."[38]

Indeed, ongoing research has found links between loneliness and health risks, particularly among older adults.[39] (Even more recent research centers on the links between mental health risks and loneliness among adolescents.)[40] The Survey Center on American Life published troubling findings about loneliness in 2021. The study showed that the proportion of people who can name six close friends has dropped from 55 percent to 27 percent since the 1990s, while people who have no close friends at all rose from 3 percent

---

35. Denworth, *Friendship*, 6.
36. Denworth, *Friendship*, 19.
37. Lewis, "Membership," 31.
38. Lewis, *Four Loves*, 87.
39. Center for Disease Control and Prevention, "Loneliness."
40. Perfas, "Young People Are Hurting."

to 12 percent. Only 59 percent of Americans have what they would describe as a best friend.[41] Perhaps, as Lewis says, "Few value it because few experience it."[42] And friendship's decreased valuation becomes part of a vicious chicken-and-egg circle in which we seek less what we value less and suffer more. There is no doubt that, as painful as the loss of Williams was to Lewis, Lewis would have agreed with Alfred, Lord Tennyson's immortal lines from *In Memoriam*, a poem mourning the loss of Tennyson's dearest friend:

> 'Tis better to have loved and lost
> Than never to have loved at all.[43]

"I CAN'T SEE THE OLD CONTOURS"

The contours of the world and the soul speak to our individuation, to the separation of night and day, earth and water, sky and firmament, person and person. Yet, the medievalist Lewis—student of the premodern world with its spheres, hierarchies, circles, descensions, and ascensions—had an eye, a mind, for the transcendent, the eternal, even the universal.

Indeed, Lewis sees friendship ultimately as serving some greater purpose than self-centered, unreciprocated need. (Aristotle distinguished among friendships rooted in utility, pleasure, and virtue. While Lewis doesn't draw out these distinctions, in *The Four Loves*, they seem implicit in his analysis of friendship as a single category.)

> The very condition of having Friends is that we should want something else besides Friends. Where the truthful answer to the question "Do you see the same truth?" would be "I see nothing and I don't care about the truth; I only want a Friend," no Friendship can arise—though Affection of course may. There would be nothing for the Friendship to be about; and Friendship must be about something, even if it were only an enthusiasm for

41. Cox, "State of American Friendship."
42. Lewis, *Four Loves*, 88.
43. Tennyson, "In Memoriam," 27.15–27.16.

dominoes or white mice. Those who have nothing can share nothing; those who are going nowhere can have no fellow-travelers.[44]

Following the death of his wife Joy Davidson, "Lewis concluded that the primary way to describe both love and friendship, is to stress the personal experience of love that transcends both."[45] Thus, Lewis writes, "Friendship exhibits a glorious 'nearness by resemblance' to Heaven itself where the very multitude of the blessed (which no man can number) increases the fruition which each has of God."[46] Such filial love, "free from instinct, free from all duties but those which love has freely assumed, almost wholly free from jealousy, and free without qualification from the need to be needed, is eminently spiritual. It is the sort of love one can imagine between angels."[47]

Shortly after Williams's death, Lewis wrote in a letter to one of his students (and a longtime correspondent):

> I also have become much acquainted with grief now through the death of my great friend Charles Williams, my friend of friends, the comforter of all our little set, the most angelic. The odd thing is that his death has made my faith ten times stronger than it was a week ago. And I find all that talk about "feeling he is closer to us than before" isn't just talk. It's just what it does feel like—I can't put it into words. One seems at moments to be living in a new world. Lots, lots of pain, but not a particle of depression or resentment.[48]

"IT'S A LARGER WORLD THAN I ONCE THOUGHT IT"

Some of Lewis's most famous insights into the nature of friendship are those that contrast *philia* with *eros*. "Lovers are always talking

---

44. Lewis, *Four Loves*, 58.
45. Scudder and Bishop, "C. S. Lewis Surprised," 74.
46. Lewis, *Four Loves*, 92–93.
47. Lewis, *Four Loves*, 111.
48. Lewis, *Books, Broadcasts, and War*, 652–53.

to one another about their love," Lewis observes. "Friends hardly ever about their Friendship. Lovers are normally face to face, absorbed in each other' Friends, side by side, absorbed in some common interest."[49] Thus, "we picture lovers face to face but Friends side by side; their eyes look ahead."[50] And "true Friendship is the least jealous of loves."[51] While lovers, as Lewis sees them, close in from the world with one another, friends look outward. The direction of such a gaze naturally reveals more of the world, not less. The phrase "a larger world" reappears as the title of part 3 of Lewis's *Poems*. Clearly, this idea is one that remained with Lewis. It echoes in a variety of ways throughout his works as a recognition that there is so much more than what is right in front of us: from the larger world that contains Narnia to the world beyond the mud pies that is a holiday at the sea.

But in Lewis, the talk of the "world" or "worlds" is never limited to the merely physical, geographical, or material. The kind of friendships Lewis writes about, experienced, and laments the loss of in this poem allow the immanent and transcendent to meet. They are both embodied in the flesh and evocative of the spirit. In other words, they point to and reflect a larger world.

Such a generous and generative concept of the world contrasts sharply with the kind of world built by those grasping for power, the kind of people Lewis described as part of the "Inner Ring." The Inner Ring is antithetical to true friendship, as Lewis defines it, although it certainly might fit into Aristotle's category of friendship based on utility. In fact, Lewis's description of the Inner Ring predicts a theory from social psychology that didn't emerge until the 1990s: the need-to-belong theory. Strong social bonds are increasingly understood as playing a role in biological processes within many species, including humans.[52] Lewis's insights into the dynamics at play in the Inner Ring reveal, then, a corruption of what is a natural, perhaps even biologically necessary, part of

---

49. Lewis, *Four Loves*, 91.
50. Lewis, *Four Loves*, 98.
51. Lewis, *Four Loves*, 92.
52. Denworth, *Friendship*, 121–37.

being human. Social bonds can be as easily—perhaps more easily—forged in fire as in love and care.

"CAUGHT IN THE BLEAK AIR THAT BLOWS ON THE RIDGE"

This phrase poignantly captures the speaker's recognition of his own vulnerability in being bereft of his friend. It is the same vulnerability, the same human proneness to the temptation to abandon virtue in favor of belonging, that Lewis captures in his essay "The Inner Ring":

> And you will be drawn in, if you are drawn in, not by desire for gain or ease, but simply because at that moment, when the cup was so near your lips, you cannot bear to be thrust back again into the cold outer world. It would be so terrible to see the other man's face—that genial, confidential, delightfully sophisticated face—turn suddenly cold and contemptuous, to know that you had been tried for the Inner Ring and rejected. And then, if you are drawn in, next week it will be something a little further from the rules, and next year something further still, but all in the jolliest, friendliest spirit. It may end in a crash, a scandal, and penal servitude; it may end in millions, a peerage and giving the prizes at your old school. But you will be a scoundrel.[53]

To be human means to be caught in a bleak air that blows at some point. But to be virtuous is to withstand the cold outer world rather than become a scoundrel. And sometimes that brings isolation, alienation, and loneliness.

"IS IT THE FIRST STING OF THE GREAT WINTER . . . OR THE COLD OF SPRING?"

With this line, one can't help but think of the great winter Lewis would write about just a few years later with his publication in

---

53. Lewis, "Inner Ring," para. 20.

1950 of *The Lion, the Witch and the Wardrobe* in which Narnia is a land beset by an endless winter. In both the poem and the novel (and more universally, of course) winter serves as a symbol of death—not the death that is an ultimate end or annihilation, but rather—like literal winter—the necessary kind of death that precedes new life, resurrection, and the eternity promised by ever-recurring spring.

The death of a friend is a death in itself (obviously), but the poem suggests that the change, the loss, rendered by that death for the speaker's life is the harbinger of both an end (the first sting of the great winter) and a beginning (spring). Death and life, like winter and spring, are hinged. This is why T. S. Eliot, in the opening line of *The Waste Land*, can refer to April as a cruel month.

"WITH WHAT FRIEND CONCERNING YOUR DEATH IS IT WORTHWHILE TO EXCHANGE THOUGHTS"

We don't choose to lose our friends (most of the time), but we especially don't when the thief is death. Yet, Lewis points out that we don't have much more power over gaining friends either, not in the grand scheme of things. (Those of us who have gone through friendless patches in life know this all too well.) Lewis explains,

> In Friendship . . . we think we have chosen our peers. In reality a few years' difference in the dates of our births, a few more miles between certain houses, the choice of one university instead of another . . . the accident of a topic being raised or not raised at a first meeting—any of these chances might have kept us apart. But, for a Christian, there are, strictly speaking no chances. A secret master of ceremonies has been at work. Christ, who said to the disciples, "Ye have not chosen me, but I have chosen you," can truly say to every group of Christian friends, "*Ye* have not chosen one another but I have chosen you for one another." The friendship is not a reward for our discriminating and good taste in finding one another

out. It is the instrument by which God reveals to each of us the beauties of others.[54]

Thus, it is within the scope of Providence that we encounter those who become our friends. Like each of our individual lives, friendship is knitted together in the womb of the world that God created and in which he has numbered our days:

> Are not all lifelong friendships born at the moment when at last you meet another human being who has some inkling (but faint and uncertain even in the best) of that something which you were born desiring, and which, beneath the flux of other desires and in all the momentary silences between the louder passions, night and day, year by year, from childhood to old age, you are looking for, watching for, listening for? You have never had it. All the things that have ever deeply possessed your soul have been but hints of it—tantalising glimpses, promises never quite fulfilled, echoes that died away just as they caught your ear. But if it should really become manifest—if there ever came an echo that did not die away but swelled into the sound itself—you would know it. Beyond all possibility of doubt you would say "Here at last is the thing I was made for."[55]

"UNLESS—OH UNLESS IT WERE YOU"

It is hard not to see echoes of Lewis's feelings for Williams expressed in this phrase of the poem in what is perhaps the most famous line from *The Four Loves*:

> Friendship arises out of mere Companionship when two or more of the companions discover that they have in common some insight or interest or even taste which the others do not share and which, till that moment, each believed to his own unique treasure (or burden). . . . "What? You too? I thought I was the only one."[56]

---

54. Lewis, *Four Loves*, 126.
55. Lewis, *Problem of Pain*, 150–51.
56. Lewis, *Four Loves*, 96.

Bibliography

Apichella, Michael. "Friendship as Philosopher: C. S. Lewis—Atheist, Deist, Christian Apologist." In *Persona and Paradox: Issues of Identity for C. S. Lewis, His Friends, and Associates*, edited by Suzanne Bray and William Gray, 106–13. Newcastle upon Tyne, UK: Cambridge Scholars, 2012.

Center for Disease Control and Prevention. "Loneliness and Social Isolation Linked to Serious Health Conditions." U.S. Department for Health & Human Services, n.d. https://www.cdc.gov/aging/publications/features/lonely-older-adults.html. Link discontinued.

Cox, Daniel A. "The State of American Friendship: Change, Challenges, and Loss." Survey Center on American Life, June 8, 2021. https://www.americansurveycenter.org/research/the-state-of-american-friendship-change-challenges-and-loss/

Denworth, Lydia. *Friendship: The Evolution, Biology, and Extraordinary Power of Life's Fundamental Bond*. New York: Norton, 2020.

Dickinson, Emily. "Tell the Truth, but Tell it Slant." In *The Poems of Emily Dickinson: Reading Edition*, edited by Ralph W. Franklin, no. 1263. Cambridge, MA: Belknap, 1998.

———. "There's a Certain Slant of Light." In *The Poems of Emily Dickinson: Reading Edition*, edited by Ralph W. Franklin, no. 320. Cambridge, MA: Belknap, 1998.

Duriez, Colin. *C. S. Lewis: A Biography of Friendship*. Oxford: Lion, 2013.

Eliot, T. S. *"The Wasteland" and Other Poems*. First Vintage Classics. New York: Vintage Classics, 2021.

Jacobs, Alan. *The Narnian: The Life and Imagination of C. S. Lewis*. New York: HarperCollins, 2005.

Kawano, Rolan M. "The Impact of Charles Williams' Death on C. S. Lewis." *Mythcon Proceedings* 1 (1971) art. 10.

Lewis, C. S. "The Alliterative Metre." In *"Rehabilitations" and Other Essays*, 117–32. London: Oxford University Press, 1939.

———. *Books, Broadcasts, and the War, 1931–1949*. Edited by Walter Hooper. Vol. 2 of *Collected Letters*. New York: HarperSanFrancisco, 2004.

———. "Dedication: To Charles Williams." In *A Preface to Paradise Lost*, v. London: Oxford University Press, 1962.

———. *The Four Loves*. New York: Harcourt, 1960.

———. "The Inner Ring." C. S. Lewis Society of California, 1944. Memorial Lecture at King's College, University of London. https://www.lewissociety.org/innerring/.

———. "Meditation in a Toolshed." In *God in the Dock: Essays on Theology and Ethics*, edited by Walter Hooper, 230–35. Grand Rapids: Eerdmans, 2014.

———. "Membership." In *"The Weight of Glory" and Other Addresses*, 30–42. New York: Macmillan, 1949.

———. *Poems*. New York: HarperOne, 1964.

———. Preface to *Essays Presented to Charles Williams*, by Dorothy Sayers et al. Oxford: Oxford University Press, 1948.

———. *The Problem of Pain*. New York: HarperOne, 1940.

———. *Surprised by Joy: The Shape of My Early Life*. New York: Harcourt Brace, 1955.

———. *"The Weight of Glory": And Other Addresses*. Rev. ed. C. S. Lewis Signature Classics. New York: HarperCollins, 2001.

McGrath, Alister. *If I Had Lunch with C. S. Lewis: Exploring the Ideas of C. S. Lewis on the Meaning of Life*. Carol Stream, IL: Tyndale, 2014.

Perfas, Samantha Layne. "Young People Are Hurting, and Their Parents Are Feeling It." *Harvard Gazette*, Mar. 6, 2023. https://news.harvard.edu/gazette/story/2023/03/worried-about-childs-mental-health-youre-not-alone/.

Raatzsch, Richard. "*Philosophical Investigations* 65ff: On Family Resemblance." Wittgenstein Archives at the University of Bergen, n.d. https://wab.uib.no/agora/tools/wab/collection-3-issue-1-article-4.annotate.

Scudder, John R., Jr., and Anne H. Bishop. "C. S. Lewis Surprised and Humanized by Joy." *Dialog* 48 (2009) 74–78. https://doi.org/10.1111/j.1540-6385.2009.00432.x.

Tennyson, Alfred, Lord. "In Memoriam A. H. H. Obiit MDCCCXXXIII: 27." Poetry Foundation, n.d. https://www.poetryfoundation.org/poems/45336/in-memoriam-a-h-h-obiit-mdcccxxxiii-27.

Time. "Religion: Theological Thriller." *Time*, Nov. 8, 1948. https://time.com/archive/6790854/religion-theological-thriller-2/.

7

Truth and Narrative

C. S. Lewis on the Atonement as a Paradigm for Careful Listening

Jane Williams

C. S. Lewis is one of the rare modern writers who is claimed by all Anglican traditions as a companion, mentor, and example. In reality, of course, Lewis was a person of a particular time, place and tradition. He was most at home in the Anglo-Catholic tradition of worship and theology, and some of his views, for example about women priests, are clearly dated; his way of life belongs to a lost world: that of the Oxbridge academic of his time. Yet those who love and admire Lewis and find him a congenial companion whatever their own place in the present Anglican world is witnessing to one of Lewis's great strengths: Lewis knew how to communicate. He was able to communicate in several different styles, appropriate to different contexts. Lewis's "profession" was as a professor of literature, in which he exercised a mastery, above all, of intelligent reading and understanding of the great variety of texts English literature draws on, and an ability to teach others how to listen carefully to what they were reading. It is those same skills that Lewis uses as a Christian apologist and disciple. Hence, he is able to put a clear, reasoned case for faith, as in *Mere Christianity*, or create a world in which faith becomes beautiful and desirable, as in the

Narnia books; he is able to write with a psychological depth, as in *A Grief Observed*, and use the power of myth to rethink our self-understanding, as in *Till We Have Faces*. He uses science fiction, with its appeal to well-loved ideas of good and evil, heroes and villains, as a call to see the battle for the world's meaning; he writes an autobiography, like Augustine of Hippo, to show how God draws the individual home through intellectual and emotional thickets. In each case, Lewis is using different techniques to achieve his ends.

This technical fluency does not make his work insincere; he is not being more "truthful" or less in each of these genres. He is simply being what he was—a person who inhabits the large world of words. Readers of Lewis will have their own favorites of his writing, and the ones they find disappointing—not "real" Lewis—as we will with any other writer or genre. In this, Lewis perhaps suffers because his readers are not all as widely read as he was himself, and because we long for heroes in our own image, only better.

But Lewis was not a hero. As more emerges of Lewis, through letters, reminiscences, and so on, it is increasingly clear that Lewis edited himself as he edited his writing. He shaped his self-narration for the task at hand. As for all of us, the "real" C. S. Lewis is known only to God, and can be told only to God: something Lewis wrote about so poignantly in *Till We Have Faces*. In his writing, there are undoubtedly areas of deliberate concealment, but also areas of edited concealment (to say nothing of unconscious concealment), attending to the question of what needs to be told in this context, for this particular end. That is not untruth, it is communication, and it may be one of the lessons Lewis has for us as Anglicans as we navigate our complex, damaged, and damaging engagement with each other. Can we learn to attend to what is being said and why, as Lewis tried to attend to what each of his works was aiming for? I have chosen particularly to examine how Lewis negotiates the communication of God's saving work in Christ, with a particular focus on the idea of atonement: what God does to annihilate the separation between humanity and God. Lewis approaches this head-on, in *Mere Christianity*, putting forward a classic, but not unproblematic, case for the atoning work of God in Christ on the cross. But he also narrates the theme of human hostility to and alienation from God, and God's response to that, in various ways, as does the Anglican tradition as a whole. Partly by historical accident, partly by design, and perhaps by providential care, the Anglican tradition has within it space for all Christians who read the Bible, say the creeds and receive the sacraments. In this, Lewis and his "method" of varied communication is very Anglican. Truth has a particular shape and character because it is God, but, also because it is God, it is perilous for any one group to believe that they alone can narrate the whole truth.[1] In the current Anglican struggles to be faithful to the truth, perhaps part of the problem is that we are telling different stories and not listening to why our stories might be different? Might C. S. Lewis help us to learn critical and patient attention again?

If we are to become the kind of readers and narrators that Lewis was and taught others to be, we also need to be self-critical. In exploring some of how Lewis interacts with the theme of atonement, we must also notice how the story we tell is inevitably partial. Sometimes that is the requirement of the narrative, as we will see in relation to Lewis's fiction. Sometimes it is a conditioning by context and culture, to which none of us is immune. But sometimes it is an unwillingness to notice that what we say in one area of our life, or our story is not compatible with what we think we believe. Lewis calls us to attentive "reading" of each other, but also to critical reading.

We start to explore Lewis's use of atonement motifs by beginning with the setting of all such work: in the nature of God.

Truth and Narrative in the Christian Formulae

The church universal does not have one single definition of salvation or how the cross of Christ affects it. It has a "definition" of God

---

1. Lewis, "Early Prose Joy," 39–40.

and a story (not fiction) to tell of how that definition calls us into being and offers itself to us.

The Creed of Nicaea says that the whole movement of the incarnation of the Son is "for our salvation" and that he was "crucified for our sake." No further elaboration is considered necessary. The Apostles' Creed, a simpler, narrative version, commits us to the gospel history of the Son's incarnation, death, resurrection, and ascension, but without gloss. The Athanasian Creed says that the Son "suffers for our salvation" and that salvation requires trust/belief in the unity of the Son with the Godhead in all things, including incarnation and crucifixion. The reasons usually given for this reticence on the part of the creeds point to the Christological controversies of the fourth and fifth centuries, with their political and theological baggage. But while the elaboration of the relation between Father and Son is undoubtedly emphatic because of the various reactions for and against Arianism and other such Christological schema, there is a more fundamental reason, which bears upon the topic of this essay. If the Son is not God, then the actions of the Son incarnate are not salvific. The creeds describe the Christian God as Father, Son, and Holy Spirit; this is the God in whom we "believe," which means "trust." If this is not so, then there is no point in any of the rest of the creeds' invitations to trust. But it is nonetheless striking that the creeds assume that once we know that in Christ we are encountering the full activity of the whole Godhead we do not then need tight definitions of concepts like "salvation" or how it is proffered by the incarnation, death, resurrection, and ascension of the Son, or instantiated in the work of the Holy Spirit in Christ's body here on earth. Implicit in this is the assumption that the presence of God is always salvific; if we know that Christ is God, then we understand that the actions of Christ are saving actions. The "truth" here is the reality of God, the Holy Trinity, who "narrates" that truth in history, in Jesus Christ and the Holy Spirit.

The usual description of what Christ achieves and what salvation means is "atonement." Whatever it is that separates us from

God is annulled by the cross.[2] This is God's own initiative, not ours, which is not surprising since we have no initiative in relation to God, but its underlying assumption is perhaps worth stating clearly: if God in Christ reaches across the divide between God and humanity, then that divide is not of God's making.

The elegant understatement of the creeds is filled out by other Christian formulae, which draw out the implications of the incarnation, death, and resurrection of Christ for Christian life, and enact this narrative in discipleship. One obvious setting for exploration of the consequences of Christ's saving work is the baptism liturgy since this is the point of entry for those who believe and trust and intend to live from that faith. The Church of England liturgy of baptism speaks of the necessity of being "born again of water and the Spirit" and that this new birth also entails a "dying to sin." The birth and death themes, renunciation for the sake of greater fulfillment, are strong, as is the interaction of themes of gift and reception, human passivity, and human activity. Baptized candidates are exhorted not to be "ashamed to confess the faith of Christ crucified," and we, the community receiving this new member, instruct them to "fight valiantly as disciples of Christ against sin, the world and the devil, and remain faithful to Christ until the end of your life."[3] In teaching on the effects of the saving work of God in Christ, I have found that description particularly useful since it avoids narrowing the "problem" to personal wrongdoing and enables a fuller understanding of the cosmic scope of salvation.

Narrating the Narrator

This baptismal framing of the problem to which God's atoning work in Christ is addressed is explicit in Lewis's autobiographical narration of his conversion. Fundamental to the unfolding of the story is Lewis's gradual realization of God's reality and

---

2. Church of England, "Lord's Supper."
3. Church of England, "Holy Baptism," s.vv. "Signing with the Cross."

distinctiveness and how this reality shapes Lewis's own story. The narrator of all is also the shaper of who we are.

Lewis describes the lures of the "world, the flesh and the devil" as ways in which human beings seek for possession, mastery of the means to "Joy." He describes the world as "the desire for glitter, swagger, distinction, the desire to be in the know."[4] The astute way in which, in *That Hideous Strength*, he describes Mark Studdock's seduction by the lure of belonging to the Progressive Element in college suggests that this temptation was the one that Lewis found most comprehensible. Although Lewis had a sturdy interest in the things of the senses and was neither a prude nor a celibate, "the flesh" does not seem to have been a serious temptation to him. In fact, he describes the "redemption" of simple pleasures like ordinary food and domestic views, and even things not at all lovely in themselves, as steps towards his final surrender. He describes this as one of the gifts bequeathed to him by his friendship with A. K. Hamilton Jenkin, who showed him "a serious, yet gleeful, determination to rub one's nose in the very quiddity of each thing, to rejoice in its being (so magnificently) what it was."[5] He is, to modern ears, extraordinarily unjudging and unperturbed by the homosexual activities at his school: nothing about it stirred him. "The chief drawback to the whole system was that it bored me considerably."[6] He does note the use and abuse of power involved in these relationships, though even there, he suggests that there was generally freedom of choice among the younger boys (to those who read Lewis after the shameful revelations of child sexual abuse and abuse of power in relation to women, Lewis's belief that a younger boy truly had freedom of choice seems naïve). Lewis notes his own physical response to, for example, a dancing mistress, but without any sense of guilt about it. This was not something against which he had to "fight valiantly."[7]

---

4. Lewis, *Surprised by Joy*, 77.
5. Lewis, *Surprised by Joy*, 231.
6. Lewis, *Surprised by Joy*, 101.
7. Church of England, "Holy Baptism," s.vv. "Signing with the Cross."

Surprised by Joy also suggests that Lewis did not find "the devil" particularly tempting, at least in the ways in which he saw the devil sought by those who dabbled in magic and the occult: "Its coarse strength betrayed it," he writes.[8] The search for "joy" that Lewis describes in this brief and selective autobiography had prepared Lewis's imagination to reject so much of what he thought of as "the world, the flesh, and the devil." Lewis distinguishes between "joy" and "pleasure"; while pleasure may be sought in various ways and places, it is an end in itself, whereas Lewis comes to realize the places where joy may be found are always ephemeral, always pointing forward, not to the emotion, the sensation that they offer, but to the thing itself: Joy. The intimations of joy, though never possessed, yet protected acceptance of anything lesser: "the Flesh and the Devil, though they could still tempt, could no longer offer me the supreme bribe. I had learned that it was not in its gift."[9] These intrinsically related creedal themes, the reality of God and how this is narrated in human lives, continue to unfold in Lewis's fiction. The "narrative" element, as in Lewis's own journey, is of God's attention to individuals and their varying degrees of resistance to and incomprehension of the way in which their story is part of God's.

In *Perelandra*, Lewis demonstrates a more subtle understanding than is found in *Surprised by Joy* of the devil's ability to tempt. There is a long section in which the devil, inhabiting the body of the scientist, Weston, attempts to bring about the fall of Perelandra.[10] The devil tries to persuade the woman that God—Maleldil—gives commands to encourage us to disobey, to grow up, to take on a more adult relationship with God and the world. The thoughts planted in the woman's mind are of her own greatness, beauty, glory, with the aim, for the devil, of opening a gap between God and the woman. She begins to think of herself as separate, with the possibility of a will, of choices, that do not flow from the simple, trustful relationship with Maleldil and the world

8. Lewis, *Surprised by Joy*, 204.
9. Lewis, *Surprised by Joy*, 204.
10. Lewis, *Perelandra*, 125–71.

she lives in. "The external and, as it were, dramatic conception of the self was the enemy's true aim. He was making her mind a theatre in which that phantom self should hold the stage. He had already written the play."[11] Where there had been one narrative of a world in which the woman lived by the loving choice of God, the woman is being tempted to tell two stories, one of which is shaped primarily by herself. This is a fictional characterization of the theological theme that Zizioulas identifies: this choice of the phantom self as the choice of "being over communion," Zizioulas's description of the fall. Human beings made for communion with God and each other choose instead to assert a selfhood that they believe to be independent; they choose self-definition first and then communion, thereby rupturing the possibility of deep, Trinitarian communion.[12] The theological narrative of *Perelandra* has the same analysis. While *Surprised by Joy* does not pursue this line of thinking in relation to Lewis himself, it provides one of the key themes in Lewis's approach to the atoning work of God and human salvation: choice, or the illusion of it that is offered by the devil.

Lewis's references to "the world, the flesh, and the devil" are what might be expected of a liturgically practiced Anglican as a means of exploring the complex layers of "sin" that require divine salvation. The creeds and the baptismal exhortations are a salutary reminder that the foundational trust is in the unity of God, giving us the certainty that the work of Christ is *pro nobis*, with all the reality of God in that gift to us. The baptism liturgies draw us away from an over-personalized understanding of atonement: not just that each "I" is reconciled to God, but that the whole world is reconciled to its creator and redeemer.

---

11. Lewis, *Perelandra*, 171.
12. Zizioulas, *Being as Communion*, 102.

Models of the Atonement in Lewis

But Lewis does also, on occasion, employ what might be called theological models of the atonement. Models and theories of the atonement seek to bring some theological imagery to help us understand or imagine the action of God in salvation. This task can be immensely fruitful; it encourages a deeper engagement with the full range of biblical texts that speak of God's saving love; it renews the wells of gratitude in Christian discipleship; it confronts us with the mysterious grace of God's action, so wholly unlike our own choices, and therefore brings us again to a fuller realization of the character of God; it engenders sorrow and humility. But, as with all God's gifts of grace to the human race, theologies of the atonement also divide. Primary emphasis on penal substitution, sacrifice, the incarnation and cross as one act, and legal acquittal are often spoken of as incompatible. They become partisan: "If you don't believe this about the cross, you are not a proper Christian." The particular narrative of atonement can become separated from its creedal basis in the nature of God, Father, Son, and Holy Spirit. Some evangelical theologians have been particularly critical of Lewis's attempt to explain the atonement in *Mere Christianity*.[13]

The task Lewis set himself in the book, which was originally a series of radio broadcasts, was to explain Christian faith to "the ordinary man" (the front cover of this edition says, "A book that makes religion exciting and stimulating for the ordinary man"),[14] avoiding denominational language and theological jargon. In the section entitled 'The Perfect Penitent,' Lewis describes his own evolving understanding of the atonement. Having started with a crude penal substitutionary view—"God wanted to punish men for having deserted and joined the Great Rebel, but Christ volunteered to be punished instead, and so God let us off"[15]—Lewis then puts forward something more akin to Anselm's theory in *Cur*

---

13. DeYoung, "Cautions for Mere Christianity."
14. Lewis, *Mere Christianity*, front cover.
15. Lewis, *Mere Christianity*, 53.

Deus Homo. "Only a bad person needs to repent: only a good person can repent perfectly."[16]

But Lewis also says, "Theories about Christ's death are not Christianity."[17] Christianity believes that the death of Christ atones, destroying the barriers that keep us from God, and that this truly happens in history. Just as scientists use mathematical formulae to describe the world without imagining that the formulae are the world itself, Christians use models of the atonement, which should not be confused with reality. From Lewis's perspective, the barriers between us and God are created by our rebellion; they are not on God's side. God does not require blood as the price of forgiveness, but humiliation and death are a description of what going back to him is like.[18] They are a necessary part of total surrender, and since we are not capable of that, God becomes human in order to do it for us. This is certainly substitutionary death, and there is certainly an element of punishment in it, though the punishment is not at God's stipulation but our need. Lewis cautions, at the end of this section, "But remember this is only one more picture. Do not mistake it for the thing itself: and if it does not help you, drop it."[19] This is a crucial statement. Do not confuse the narrative and the Narrator.

In *Perelandra* the question is approached differently because the context is different. The *Cosmic Trilogy* is primarily what might be called science fiction: it tells a story, and story and theological ideas serve each other. *Perelandra* is a planet whose destiny is interconnected with all others, though that connection is unknown in the Silent Planet, Earth. Yet the history of Earth—Thulcandra— has the potential to warp that of Perelandra as Weston, the human scientist, has allowed himself to become the carrier of the evil one, who increasingly digests Weston.[20] Ransom is called upon to fight Weston, now the "Un-man," to the death to prevent the fall

16. Lewis, *Mere Christianity*, 56; Anselm, *Cur Deus Homo*.
17. Lewis, *Mere Christianity*, 54.
18. Lewis, *Mere Christianity*, 56.
19. Lewis, *Mere Christianity*, 58.
20. Lewis, *Perelandra*, 217.

of Perelandra. As he realizes this is necessary, the Voice—Christ—reminds him, with inexorable irony, that Christ, too, could be known as "Ransom." Ransom understands that if this planet, too, falls, this planet, too, will be redeemed; its ransom will be paid, not by crucifixion, because Maleldil never repeats, but its redemption, like that of Earth, will be shockingly costly. In a chilling moment, Ransom confronts the possessed Weston with the atonement—the way in which God made some good from the fall of Earth. He reminds Weston that when Maleldil went to a human death for Earth's redemption, it was not the defeat of Maleldil that ensued, as the Evil One had expected. Even in defeat, the Un-man in Weston's body continues to remember, with vicious joy, as a treasured possession, Jesus' cry from the cross, "My God, my God, why have you forsaken me." The Un-man cannot begin to grasp the depth of humiliation to which Maleldil will go in self-sacrificial love, if Perelandra, too, needs to be ransomed.[21]

The *Cosmic Trilogy* uses an atonement narrative of the conflict between good and evil. It allows a powerful imaginative depiction of the fundamental difference in character between these two forces. Evil, both in *Perelandra* and in *That Hideous Strength*, possesses people, Weston and the Head, but it is never incarnate; it does not share the reality of what it possesses, merely uses it for its own ends.[22] Evil is repetitive, unlike good. Good never does the same thing twice, but evil tries to recreate the fall of Earth on Perelandra. The vicious, petty, nastiness of Screwtape and his nephew, Wormwood, their disdain and disgust for human beings, is depicted in the *Cosmic Trilogy*, without the dark humor to alleviate it.[23] As in *The Screwtape Letters*, so in the *Cosmic Trilogy*, Lewis brings out the fundamentally different character of good and evil. Screwtape is, ultimately, delighted by the failure of his nephew, and looks forward to consuming him;[24] the people drawn to NICE in *That Hideous Strength* are all there to feed their own

---

21. Lewis, *Perelandra*, 149, 190.
22. Lewis, *Screwtape Letters*, 15.
23. Lewis, *Screwtape Letters*, preface.
24. Lewis, *Screwtape Letters*, 68.

needs and passions and, as Mark quickly discovers, there is no loyalty or kindness to be found in any of them. In contrast, the good across the interplanetary world are a community of love and respect, wanting only what enables the flourishing of others, wanting only the fulfillment of Maleldil's will. The little community around Ransom, too, display faithfulness and tolerance towards each other, despite differences in character and priorities.

That Hideous Strength ends with the grotesquely violent destruction of those who have chosen evil, and an equally grotesque series of scenes of sexual love for those who have chosen the good. This is not the end of all things, as described in *The Last Battle*, but a stage on the way, a clear demonstration that evil eats its children without compunction and therefore cannot last.

The way in which Ransom physically fights and kills the possessed Weston, and the slaughter of the evil company in *That Hideous Strength* are perhaps a strand of Lewis's narration that an attentive and critical reader might want to challenge. The one who names himself as also a ransom to Ransom before the fight very deliberately chose not to fight physically and rebuked his disciples for their attempts to do so (Luke 22:51). The ransom Jesus pays is his own life, and although Ransom knows that his death is possible in the fight, nonetheless, he fights to win a physical battle over evil. Yet earlier, as already quoted, Lewis says that if Perelandra falls, it too will be redeemed by "some act of even more appalling love, some glory of yet deeper humility." And in *Mere Christianity* Lewis has argued that Jesus' human death is done on our behalf, because only in surrender and humility can we approach God. There is an apparent disconnect in Lewis's theology here: God incarnate does not choose to redeem through violence, but human beings who are called into the service of this God may need to fight violently? It is as though Lewis does not quite believe his own theological logic. Yet it is a crucial—the word is apt—point for any narrating of the atonement: the crucifixion is "the power of God and the wisdom of God," though a "stumbling block to Jews and foolishness to Gentiles" (1 Cor 1:23-24).[25] It does not make human sense that

---

25. Scripture quotation in this chapter is from the NRSV.

this is the way in which God redeems humanity; the challenge to human perceptions of power and success is overwhelming and remains unpalatable foolishness, even to sincere followers of Christ. Lewis appears to be saying that God may act in one way. However, human beings are still validated to act in a way that is not in accord with the character of God as displayed in Jesus Christ, "the image of the invisible God" (Col 1:15), who "humbled himself and become obedient to the point of death—even death on the cross" (Phil 2:8).

Perhaps it is possible to argue that this is not Lewis's own theological position but a necessity of the fictional narrative he is telling. Still, *Perelandra* is one of the most explicitly theological of Lewis's fictional works, making it harder to see this as anything other than a genuine theological disjunction in Lewis's thinking.

In another of Lewis's fictional works, the incomplete use of a "theory of the atonement" does seem to be deliberate and to serve the narrative. In *The Lion, the Witch and the Wardrobe*, Lewis returns directly to atonement theology and, once again, it is important to notice context. Like the *Cosmic Trilogy*, this is fiction. There are unfinished edges in logic because logic is not the point, narrative is. As with the *Cosmic Trilogy*, the Narnia stories depict a series of interdependent worlds, where the fate of one affects what happens in others. It is an evil from our world that brings evil to Narnia;[26] children from our world play key roles in the providential care of Narnia; Aslan is known by another name in our world, but is recognizable in character, attributes, and action.

Aslan gives himself into the hands of the witch in payment—ransom—for Edmund. This is the Deep Magic written into Narnia from the dawn of time. This is the kind of magic the witch knows because she, too, is a creature of time. But Aslan explains that there is something deeper, which comes from before all time. The self-giving of an innocent one, who offers themselves in place of the guilty, triggers a completely new reaction, older and deeper than the one the witch knows. The victim bound on the table will be

---

26. See Lewis, *Magician's Nephew*.

free, and death will be undone.²⁷ *The Magician's Nephew* shows that Aslan envisages the necessity for this self-giving from the dawn of Narnia's history, already tainted by the presence of Jadis.²⁸ As with Ransom's fight with the Un-man in *Perelandra*, so in *The Lion, the Witch and the Wardrobe*, the ransom—though this time of Aslan's willingness to be humbled, defeated, and die—is decisive in relation to this particular crisis in the narrative, but it is not ultimate. The witch is defeated and apparently dead by the end of the story but she, or some manifestation of her, will return; evil needs to be defeated by human choice, over and over again in Lewis's fictional world. Otherwise, there would be no story. This is not a theological textbook, but a fictional world in which readers can see the beauty and power of Christian themes.²⁹

The Lion, the Witch and the Wardrobe is using a variation of a "model of the atonement" that is most akin to that put forward by Gregory of Nyssa in "The Catechetical Oration":

> In order to secure that the ransom in our behalf might be easily accepted by him who required it, the Deity was hidden under the veil of our nature, that so, as with ravenous fish, the hook of the Deity might be gulped down along with the bait of flesh, and thus, life being introduced into the house of death, and light shining in darkness, that which is diametrically opposed to light and life might vanish.³⁰

The devil, like the White Witch, is deceived by its own greedy eagerness and ignorance, though in *The Lion, the Witch and the Wardrobe*, the witch is not deceived about who Aslan is. In Nyssa's proposition, the devil cannot see beyond the humanity of Jesus to his divinity, but in Narnia, Aslan does not hide his nature.

This is the image of the atonement that is most usually cited in relation to Lewis; but it is worth noting that in this narrative it is only Edmund's "sin" that is atoned for by the death of Aslan.

27. Lewis, *Lion, Witch, Wardrobe*, 176.
28. Lewis, *Magician's Nephew*, 80.
29. Lewis, *Mere Christianity*, 63.
30. "Catechetical Oration" 24, in Gregory of Nyssa, *Dogmatic Treatises*.

Although the magic is written into the world from the dawn of time, we see it in operation only here, in this particular story. Logically, it might then be possible that Aslan would have to die again, should another traitor be in need of salvation; but that conclusion mistakes the narrative setting of this "theory of the atonement." Readers see the depth of God's love, willing to die for even one sinner, and that is the emotional heart of Aslan's death on the Stone Table. It gives us insight into the truth of the love of God in Christ Jesus, which avails not just for one Edmund, but for all. Michael Ramsey writes, "The infinite worth of the one is the key to the Christian understanding of the many,"[31] and this is what Aslan's death for Edmund shows us: a close-up of the love of God.

There are also signs in *The Lion, the Witch and the Wardrobe* of a wider view of the redeeming work of God not just for the individual but for the whole of creation. Aslan's power is at work against the witch's evil in other ways. The "incarnation," the coming of Aslan into Narnia, begins the onslaught on the power of the White Witch. Her winter begins to thaw once it is rumored that Aslan is on the move.[32] Athanasius's great work, *De incarnatione verbi*, holds the incarnation and death of Jesus as one great, saving act, dealing with the corruption introduced into creation through sin, which leads to the death and decay of what God has made, and therefore calls into question God's original self-giving in creation. Athanasius writes,

> What—or rather Who was it that was needed for such grace and such recall as we required? Who, save the Word of God Himself, Who also in the beginning had made all things out of nothing? His part it was, and His alone, both to bring again the corruptible to incorruption and to maintain for the Father His consistency of character with all. For He alone, being Word of the Father and above all, was in consequence both able to

---

31. Michael Ramsey, in Rowell et al., *Love's Redeeming Work*, 666.
32. Lewis, *Lion, Witch, Wardrobe*, 116–26.

recreate all, and worthy to suffer on behalf of all and to be an ambassador for all with the Father.[33]

Within loosely Protestant churches, there has perhaps been a tendency to separate the work of creation and the work of atonement in a way that is not upheld by, for example, John 1 or Colossians 1, which, like Athanasius, assume that it is because the Son is the source of creation that the Son can also be its savior.

In Lewis's fiction and nonfiction approaches to the atonement, the point Lewis is interested in making is that the death of Christ is decisive, but that the world remains "enemy-occupied territory,"[34] and human beings are still given the choice of whether to side with the occupier or the rightful king. Christians are given three things to keep God's new life in Christ growing in us, according to Lewis: baptism, belief, and Holy Communion.[35] Lewis is clear about what is achieved by the death of Christ and what is still to come: "His death has washed out our sins, and . . . by dying He disabled death itself."[36] The occupied territory will be reclaimed, in totality, after this period of grace in which human choice is still operative.

It is human choice that is the primary focus of most of Lewis's writing about salvation, though the balance between human and divine action is always carefully nuanced. Lewis is a powerful analyst of human character and motive: Edmund and Eustace are not just willfully wrong in their initial bad choices but also conditioned by all kinds of influences beyond their entire control. The bitter Queen Orual has had bitterness thrust upon her, however willingly she accepts it.[37] Lewis himself, in *Surprised by Joy*, describes his own resistance to God, and the factors that conditioned that resistance. In each case, choice is both free and yet conditioned; people make a choice for God but find that God has also made a choice for them. God's grace is "prevenient"—human choice is not

---

33. Athanasius, *Incarnation* 2.7.
34. Lewis, *Mere Christianity*, 47.
35. Lewis, *Mere Christianity*, 59.
36. Lewis, *Mere Christianity*, 55.
37. Lewis, *Till We Have Faces*.

left to serendipity but is already informed by God's grace. There is a story to be told about every individual, but it is also, and always, a story about the whole of creation and its relationship to God.

Conclusion

The main point of this paper is the sheer fun of rereading Lewis and noting his narrative and psychological skills. But the argument, insofar as there is one, is that, within the broad scope of creedal and baptismal theology, Lewis expects us to attend to context, to what the story is actually about. Creeds and liturgy are generous in their boundaries, but the boundaries are real. They may not prescribe one required model of God's action in Christ, but they do require assent to the reality and decisiveness of that action.

Those of us who teach "models of the atonement" can fall into the trap of choosing a model that fits appropriately for a particular culture, how it sees "sin" and therefore what it assumes redemption entails. This can be helpful, and can enable us to see that, in one sense, all the models have evolved to address real people in real historical settings. But it can also blind us to the fact that one of the many things that the atonement shows us is that we don't know ourselves well or diagnose our needs at all accurately. Overwhelmingly, such teaching and preaching as there is on the atonement in churches now focuses on God's love reaching out for us in our alienation. Of course, that is what God does, but that description does not enable a theology of the cross—why does Jesus have to die for the love of God to reach us?

Lewis's approach is, in one sense, to choose a description of the action of God that is appropriate to the narrative he is telling, fictional, descriptive, or autobiographical. But its great strength is in requiring the reader to pay attention to a specific dramatic narrative, not just a generalized cultural context. In each case, the reader must ask: Who is this written for? What has led to this, and what will its consequences be? Why is this the form in which human and divine action play out in this particular narrative? Orual pours out her accusation to the gods, and as she does so, she realizes that she has been lying to herself: she has not been simply a victim; she has had agency, which she has frequently misused. Edmund and Eustace realize that they have not just been treated as outsiders by the selfish and uncomprehending world but have made themselves outsiders by their untruthfulness and greed. Repeatedly, at the heart of what might be seen as the "conversion" of a fictional character is the moment when the divine enables the human to tell the truth, not their own preferred version of it. Lewis writes, "I had hoped that the heart of reality might be of such a kind that we can best symbolize it as a place; instead, I found it to be a Person."[38] God is not impersonal and does not deal with us impersonally.

It is highly unlikely that this methodology of attention to person, context, and narrative will provide a theological breakthrough in disputes. But it is nonetheless worth suggesting that many theological disputes operate as though God were an impersonal "absolute," unable to see or attend to our reality. In response to this kind of "absolute," we become unable to attend to each other. Careful attention, as it operates in Lewis, is not situation ethics: it does not say that God and God's character adapts to us. On the contrary, it suggests we can only adapt to God when "we have faces." This is then, in the end, perhaps a call to us to show each other our faces, to tell our stories, as we see them. As with Lewis, so with each one of us, and each community, the stories we tell will be consciously and unconsciously edited. Like Orual, only God can help us see the whole truth, in that place of supreme love which is judgement. But that does not relieve us of the responsibility of attending to each other and trying to see what story is being told, particularly in our disagreements. The context of the story may be racism, colonialism, mistreatment of women, or homosexual people; it may be a story of defending Scripture or tradition, or of trying to be faithful to the witness of saints and martyrs, the great cloud of witnesses with whom we share a faith that is not ours alone. The list of possible framings is long, but not always well attended to.

---

38. Lewis, *Surprised by Joy*, 268.

Again, as we have tried to do with our attention to Lewis in this paper, even as we try to listen well, with respect and love, to different stories, we may be called to challenge. Few of us have a "systematic theology" that is actually fully systematic, without breaks in logic that have the potential to undermine vital witness to the character of God. It is not our calling to mark the lives of others as we might an essay in systematic theology. Still, it is our calling to refine and be refined by our interaction, in pain and in blessing, in the body of Christ, and to allow the great Narrator to weave what seemed separate into a whole.

Bibliography

Anselm. *Cur Deus Homo (Why God Became Man)*. Fordham University, 1998. Internet Medieval Sourcebook. From *St. Anselm: Proslogium; Monologium: An Appendix in Behalf of "The Fool" by Gaunilo; and Cur Deus Homo*, translated by Sidney Norton Deane (Repr., Chicago: Open Court, 1926). Etext from the Christian Classics Ethereal Library, here modernized in some spellings. https://sourcebooks.fordham.edu/basis/anselm-curdeus.asp#ACHAPTER%20V.

Athanasius. *On the Incarnation of the Word*. CCEL, n.d. https://www.ccel.org/ccel/athanasius/incarnation.iii.html.

Church of England. "Holy Baptism." Church of England, n.d. From *Common Worship*. https://www.churchofengland.org/prayer-and-worship/worship-texts-and-resources/common-worship/christian-initiation/holy-baptism-5.

———. "The Lord's Supper or Holy Communion." Church of England, n.d. From *Book of Common Prayer*. https://www.churchofengland.org/prayer-and-worship/worship-texts-and-resources/book-common-prayer/lords-supper-or-holy-communion.

DeYoung, Kevin. "Cautions for Mere Christianity." Gospel Coalition, Jan. 28, 2011. https://www.thegospelcoalition.org/blogs/kevin-deyoung/cautions-for-mere-christianity/.

Gregory of Nissa. *Dogmatic Treatises*. CCEL, n.d. From *Nicene and Post-Nicene Fathers*, 2nd ser., edited by Philip Schaff, vol. 5. https://www.ccel.org/ccel/schaff/npnf205.xi.ii.xxvi.html.

Lewis, C. S. "'Early Prose Joy': C. S. Lewis's Early Draft of an Autobiographical Manuscript." *VII: Journal of the Marion E. Wade Center* 30 (2013) 13–50. https://www.jstor.org/stable/48599471.

———. *The Lion, the Witch and the Wardrobe*. New York: HarperCollins, 1950.

———. *The Magician's Nephew*. New York: HarperCollins, 1955.

———. *Mere Christianity*. London: Fontana, 1959.

———. *Perelandra*. Vol. 2 of *The Cosmic Trilogy*. New York: HarperCollins, 2003.

———. *The Screwtape Letters*. New York: HarperOne, 1942.

———. *Surprised by Joy: The Shape of My Early Life*. New York: Harcourt, Brace, Jovanovich, 1955.

———. *That Hideous Strength*. Vol. 3 of *The Cosmic Trilogy*. New York: HarperCollins, 2005.

———. *Till We Have Faces: A Myth Retold*. New York: HarperOne, 1956.

Rowell, Geoffrey, et al., eds. *Love's Redeeming Work: The Anglican Quest for Holiness*. Oxford: Oxford University Press, 2003.

Zizioulas, John. *Being as Communion*. London: Darton, Longman & Todd, 1985.

www.ingramcontent.com/pod-product-compliance
Lightning Source LLC
Chambersburg PA
CBHW071331190426
43193CB00041B/1493